# MANAGEMENT OF TOMORROW

# HISTORY OF MANAGEMENT THOUGHT

# MANAGEMENT OF TOMORROW

## L[yndall] Urwick

ARNO PRESS
A New York Times Company
New York • 1979

63880

*Publisher's Note:* This book has been reproduced from the best available copy.

Editorial Supervision: BRIAN QUINN
Reprint Edition 1979 by Arno Press Inc.

Reprinted from a copy in the Library of the University of Illinois

HISTORY OF MANAGEMENT THOUGHT
    AND PRACTICE
ISBN for complete set: 0-405-12306-X
See last pages of this volume for titles.

Manufactured in the United States of America

―――――

**Library of Congress Cataloging in Publication Data**

Urwick, Lyndall Fownes, 1891-
    Management of tomorrow.

    (History of management thought)
    Reprint of the ed. published by Nisbet,
London.
    Includes index.
    1.  Industrial management.  I.  Title.
II.  Series.
HD31.U756  1979      658.4      79-7558
ISBN 0-405-12344-2

# MANAGEMENT OF TOMORROW

# MANAGEMENT OF TOMORROW

BY

## L. URWICK

O.B.E., M.C., M.A.

DIRECTOR, INTERNATIONAL MANAGEMENT INSTITUTE,
GENEVA

LONDON: NISBET AND CO., LTD.
22 BERNERS STREET, W.1

*First published in 1933*

Made and Printed in Great Britain

## PREFACE

SOME portions of the subject-matter of different chapters of this book have formed the basis
of addresses to the British Association for the
Advancement of Science, the International Association for Industrial Relations, the International
Association for Commercial Education, the Institute
of Public Administration, the Business Research and
Management Association, the Incorporated Sales
Managers Association, the Management Research
Groups and the Industrial Lecture Conferences
organised by Mr. B. S. Rowntree. The author is
also indebted to the International Chamber of
Commerce, to Sir·Isaac Pitman & Sons, Ltd., and
to The Sylvan Press for permission to draw upon
material published under their auspices.

The book was suggested by his friend and
colleague Mr. G. E. Milward, Secretary of the
Management Library, and his publishers have given
substantial help in its arrangement.

# CONTENTS

## *Part Four*

### TRAINING FOR MANAGEMENT

# INTRODUCTION

THIS book brings together and recasts in connected form material which has resulted from investigations extending over a number of years. Each of the subjects included deals with some special aspect of the management of business enterprises. But they are all linked by a common approach to the different specific problems involved. It is an approach which has been described, for lack of a better term, as " scientific ". To avoid misunderstanding, however, it should be made clear from the beginning that the management of aggregations of human beings for any purpose cannot at present, or for a long time to come, be treated as an exact science in the sense that mathematics or physics are exact sciences. It is, and will remain, an art or craft.

Where large masses of human beings are concerned knowledge of the standard of precision called for by the exact sciences is lacking. There is, however, the widest possible difference between an art or craft which is practised with due regard for the scientific knowledge which is available and in the scientific temper in relation to unknown or uncertain factors, and an art or craft which is wholly empirical, traditional and individual in methods and outlook. It is the difference between modern medical practice and the efforts of the barber-surgeons of the sixteenth century.

There is, of course, no novelty in the idea that a scientific approach to the problems of business management will prove more profitable to the individual enterprise than the older traditional techniques. Before 1900 F. W. Taylor had published the results of experiments in the organisation of production which formed the basis of the conceptions which are described collectively as " Scientific Management ". But the controversies which have since raged round Taylor's words and work, and round the application of scientific criteria to wider economic issues, all go to prove how hardly men accept the real implications of Taylor's philosophy.

Business men as a whole are willing and anxious to borrow the improvements in detailed method which result from scientific study. But they conceive of these improvements as extraneous facilities which may be adapted to their requirements within the framework of current business traditions and structure. They are less willing to admit that science is a method of thought which cannot be applied piecemeal, that it postulates a logic which must permeate ultimately every aspect of humanity's economic activity, as it has already permeated the materials and processes and many of the methods of production.

Since Taylor's death in 1915 two parallel and complementary developments have taken place.

Students of Taylor's work have extended his basic conception of the scientific approach to a range of new problems concerned with the management of the individual concern. In the case of the most advanced scientific management undertakings these experiments have today covered virtually the whole field. Not only production-shop organisation, but office methods, purchasing, finance and accountancy, selling and marketing, personnel control, and finally general organisation and administration have each been brought under the microscope. The volume of recorded experience is not at present sufficient for the enunciation of established principles covering the whole of each of these aspects of management. But instances are available with reference to nearly any single problem of experiments properly analysed, measured and controlled. The amount of conscious, objective, scientific management work grows yearly. There is an increasing appreciation of the possibility and value of comparison between the methods and results of different undertakings.

More recently, and in the larger field of relations between enterprises in the same trade, between producers and various types of distributors, between interdependent industries, and with reference to national economies viewed as a whole and to world economy, the possibility of applying the same scientific point of view has made progress under the general title of Rationalisation. Originating as a national movement under the stimulus of the German effort for economic rehabilitation in the years from 1922 to 1925, it was associated with scientific management and with a number of other parallel movements possessing the same general significance by the resolutions of the World Economic Conference of 1927. Those resolutions focussed the whole work hitherto accomplished in seeking to eliminate by objective study the manifest and obvious wastes in the current economic system.[1]

The events of the last four years have both retarded and hastened that process. In so far as the political results of the decade following the war have increased uncertainty and apprehension among different racial and national groups, emotions have been released which are inimical to objective discussion of any economic issue. In so far as unemployment has followed on business depression resulting from political intransigeance and mutual distrust, efforts at better organisation tend to be discounted as likely to displace labour. In the degree to which nations have sought for individual and exclusive protection against the storm by tariff barriers, currency restrictions and similar measures, antagonisms have been hardened and the possibility of reasonable mutual arrangements has decreased.

On the other hand the very severity of the crisis has forced a general revision of economic thinking. It has become increasingly apparent

[1] Cf. the author's *The Meaning of Rationalisation*, London : Nisbet & Co., 1929, for a general description of the movement in 1929.

that a mere rationalisation of the means of production, unaccompanied by any deliberate and scientific organisation of the mechanisms of distribution and of finance, will merely aggravate the disorder. While current political tendencies are markedly nationalistic, they have also in many instances increased the stability of national governments and thus the possibility of international economic arrangements.

Most important of all, perhaps, the long continued depression has forced the chiefs of business enterprises in all countries to devote increasing attention to the elements of efficiency. Scientific methods of management are in practice the most economical and the most effective. Thus a preparation of minds has been taking place, where such preparation was most important and where, in the long run, it is likely to prove most influential.

The necessity for such a development is overwhelming. The paradox presented by the present condition of the world's economic affairs is both unprecedented and intolerable. It is unprecedented because for the first time the world community can produce its requirements. Of that there is no question. It is intolerable because men and women have changed. There are greater general knowledge and wider expectations of life which cynicism may easily ferment into despair and disorder. Broadly speaking, large populations have become at the same time and for the first time intercommunicating and economically conscious.

The possibility of a far wider application of scientific method is equally manifest. But such application has been almost universally limited to the productive processes and to the materials and methods of manufacture. Applications to the mechanism of distribution have been few and scattered, applications to the mechanism of finance negligible. The present situation is therefore what an impartial visitor from another planet might logically anticipate. For over 100 years humanity has been subjecting to an unparalleled and intensive development one-third of the total cycle of its business activities. The remaining two-thirds have been left to hazard, to the play of forces.

The probability that the world community will accept this scientific approach is less certain:

" Most of those civilisations or peoples that have had a long history have from time to time been brought up against an imperative call to revise their scheme of institutions in the light of their native instincts, on pain of collapse or decay. . . . But history records more frequent and more spectacular instances of the triumph of imbecile institutions over life and culture, than of peoples who have by force of instinctive insight saved themselves alive out of a desperately precarious institutional situation, such, for instance, as now faces the peoples of Christendom." [1]

It is significant that these phrases were written early in 1914.

Those best qualified to speak are at least

[1] Thorstein Veblen, *The Instinct of Workmanship*, pp. 24 and 25.

emphatic as to the need for such a recasting of ideas.[1] "The mental revolution" of which F. W. Taylor spoke with reference to machine-shop management, must prevail not only in the conduct of individual business enterprises under the existing economic system, but in relation to that system itself, to public administration, to government, to politics, and to international affairs. Either that or our civilisation will go down in chaos under the weight of a material production which we are unable to control.

But to the majority, new conceptions come gradually and most easily in relation to the detail of their daily lives. For the author the general idea of rationalisation, of a scientific management which might transcend the immediate limitations of competitive *laisser-faire*, was developed over a period of years largely as the result of contact with immediate industrial problems. It is possible that the story of this evolution may be of some service. Hence this book.

[1] Cf. "We meet with great and unexpected accidents like the Great War. We shall go on having such accidents as long as our rulers are not merely ignorant of science, but think on pre-scientific lines. . . . We have got to learn to think scientifically, not only about inanimate things, but about ourselves and one another."—J. B. S. Haldane, *The Inequality of Man.*

"The age in which we live is scientific. Its problems call for fearless and original scientific thought if it is to survive and triumph. It has been left too long in peril of shipwreck— at the mercy of mediaeval and obsolete ideas."—Frederick Soddy, *Money versus Man.*

# PART ONE

## THE SCIENTIFIC APPROACH
## TO BUSINESS MANAGEMENT

### I

" So far is the machine process from having yet recast the principles of industrial management, as distinct from technological procedure, that the efforts inspired in responsible public officials and public-spirited citizens by this patent discrepancy have hitherto been directed wholly to regulating industry into consonance with the antiquated scheme of business principles, rather than to take thought how best to conduct industrial affairs and the distribution of livelihood in consonance with the technical requirements of the machine industry."—THORSTEIN VEBLEN, *The Instinct of Workmanship*.

# CHAPTER I

## THE OLD AND THE NEW IN BUSINESS

IN dealing with changes in the theory and practice of that part of business activity which is known as management, those changes must be related to the developments which have occurred in industry itself as a whole. If new methods are required for the discharge of what appear to be old tasks, it is because the tasks themselves have changed. The new methods are enforced by a new situation.

The industrial situation has altered profoundly during the last fifty years. There has been tremendous growth in the size of the industrial undertaking, the individual factory or unit of production. This is a matter on which it is exceedingly difficult to give adequate statistics. It is the commonly accepted view of economists that in every trade there is a particular size of industrial unit which gives the most efficient results, and that for different kinds of trades this ideal size varies very considerably. And in any one trade the size may vary at different levels of the task of management. That is to say one size of unit may give the best results and conduce to the highest efficiency where the financial control and the

3

purchase of raw materials is concerned, another size of unit may be better for the actual productive processes. Thus a great firm such as Courtauld's may have a centralised financial control and many different factories. But though there are many factors making for the survival of small businesses in special cases : " in finance, transport, mining, the major branches of staple manufacture, and the distribution of necessary goods and services in large towns, the economy of large business prevails, and the general drift has been towards an ever-increasing size ".

American experience is even more striking. A recent article says :

" A few years ago a plant employing 1,000 men was considered a large concern. Today factories employing 5,000 men are common, factories employing 10,000 men are not unusual, and a few plants have employed as many as 25,000 men within the confines of a single yard."

There has been development also in the composition of the industrial unit. This development has been both vertical and lateral. Industries engaged in different processes of the same trade have combined in order to eliminate transportation costs, and to meet competition by economies in administration and the elimination of intermediate profits and risks. Today many great steel producers own their own coal-mines and their own steamships. The acquirement by the Ford enterprises of their own mines, and railways, smelting plant, and lumber concessions is a good example of this development. On the other hand, firms engaged on the same process have combined laterally in order to control prices and markets and access to raw materials. The Lever combine and the Imperial Tobacco Company are instances of this form of growth.

There have been, too, very rapid and striking changes in the legal forms under which the ownership and control of industrial enterprises have been exercised. Where fifty years ago most undertakings were carried on under individual private ownership or by partnerships, today this method is the exception, representing only about 10 per cent. of the whole industrial and commercial enterprise of Great Britain. This tendency to incorporation is equally evident in other countries in an advanced stage of industrial development. The ownership and control of the producing unit is passing, has in fact very largely passed, from a personal to an impersonal basis, from the influence of individuals who stake their all on an enterprise, in which they usually assume an active share of the management, to the more remote administration of boards of Directors representing or assumed to represent the widely scattered interests of large bodies of shareholders.

A somewhat similar tendency to alteration in the forms of ownership and control is noticeable in the very large increase of public enterprises performing services or carrying on commercial activities. Municipal tramways or electricity enterprises are a case in point, while in the same class

fall those semi-public enterprises which are adminis-
tered by trustees or other *ad hoc* bodies, such as the
Port of London authority, the Bank of England,
or the new Marketing Boards.  A further diversity
and change in methods of control is offered by the
growth of the Co-operative movement.

There is an increasing complexity of relationships between the industrial unit and the groups
in contact with it.

There are, first of all, international relations.
The present disorders of Europe in themselves call
attention to the enormous amount of formal and
informal regulation to which the expanding international commerce of the nineteenth century gave
rise.  Apart from his ordinary commercial dealings
the manufacturer is today brought into touch with
international action in many directions.  He cannot afford for instance to neglect the establishment
of the International Labour Office at Geneva,
either as regards the very important work it is at
present doing in the direction of investigation and
report, or in its implications for the future, should
the League of Nations succeed in consolidating its
position as a definite international authority.  He
is concerned with such matters as international
arbitration agreements, trade exhibitions of international scope, or such gatherings as meetings of
the Chambers of Commerce of the world.

Secondly, relations with the State are constantly expanding both in scope and in detail.
Since 1900, we have had in Great Britain the
consolidated factory acts of 1901 and the Trade

Boards Act of 1909. No attempt to dismiss these tendencies irritably as "interference" can evade the fact that the community has an increasingly tender conscience as to the conditions under which its needs shall be satisfied.

Relationships between the industrial unit and the local authority of the area in which it operates are constantly expanding. In building, in education, in questions of rating, often in the transport of its employees, or in matters of water or electricity supply, it is vitally interested in the character and efficiency of the local government.

Contacts between competitors in the same trade have also increased enormously in the last decade. Both spontaneously, and as a result of government action, the numbers of employers' and trade associations have grown a hundredfold. The scope of their activities is constantly widening. The Committee on Trusts reported in 1919, " There is at the present time in every important branch of industry in the United Kingdom an increasing tendency towards the formation of trade associations and combinations."

The growth of the trade union movement, and its assumption of national responsibilities in many trades has brought about a new range of relationships between the industrial unit and those who work in it.

There has been a very rapid and important evolution of the assistant factors which good management must use, which have indeed become the commonplace of any well-conducted works.

There is the whole group of specialised skills released by the mathematical and physical sciences. The Works Engineer is a comparatively old-established institution : yet it is common knowledge that his science is in process of constant refinement and subdivision. Chemistry has replaced craftsmanship over large areas of industry, and according to the special nature of the product has its counterpart in metallurgy, physics, and other sciences. Accountancy has made enormous strides within living memory, and in statistics and costing has begotten two lusty children, neither of whom will tolerate indifference.

No less important are those sciences and movements which are designed to help the manager in dealing with the human factors in production. The Welfare movement has called attention to the importance of medical, optical and dental clinics, and the study of specialised employment methods. Psychology is rapidly claiming a definite place in the solution of a large proportion of the direct problems in dealing with subordinates. Physiology is constantly increasing the field in which it is enabled to pronounce on factors affecting efficiency.

Thus in five fundamental features—size, composition, method of ownership and control, relationships to other groups, and variety of knowledge used—there has been a rapid and profound change in the industrial unit during the last fifty years.

Each of these changes affects the task of management.

The effect of size is fairly obvious. It is a

commonplace that the old intimate personal touch between the responsible control and the men at the bench is gone. This may or may not be a matter for regret. What subordinates want is neither brutality nor kindness, but justice. And justice between man and man is the fruit of good organisation informed by a profound sense of equality. Such organisation must be based on principles rather than on any personal impulse however lofty. The " personal touch " sometimes issues in personal touchiness. Whatever the individual's views on this question, the growth in the size of the industrial unit has profoundly altered the scope of the task of management, and this applies to all grades.

The alteration in the composition of businesses places the manager at a distance from his results and has effects no less important because they are more subtle and less obvious. The existence of a chain of businesses dealing in the same or similar products—a lateral integration as it is called— forces upon the individual manager a new attitude towards his product. The immediate test of profitable production on the individual line ceases to be of the same importance. While the principles of economy and efficiency have still to be observed, it may be sound business to produce a single line or even the whole of the products of a particular factory at a loss in order to support a market or to hold out a competitor. The immediate commercial significance of each transaction is denied the manager under such circumstances. The discipline of £ s. d. is removed one or several stages. Similarly where several factories are engaged on successive processes—vertical integration—there is a call for precision in delivery and a continuing interest of the whole concern in the particular product after it has left the individual works, unknown to the management of the past.

Changes in the form of the ownership and control of business enterprises require somewhat more detailed treatment. What are the essential features of a corporation as distinct from a private concern? It is an association. It stands for a group activity. The manager is the servant not of this individual or of that, but of a group. Loyal and disinterested service to the group is both a harder, and a more worthy task, than individual fealty. The two loyalties differ as feudal loyalty differs from loyalty to a democratic state.

A corporation is by its very being a creature of the State. It is incorporated by the will and under the laws of the community. From those laws it derives its ultimate authorisation. And however much it may serve private interests in the immediate act, " the corporation is authorised by the State on the assumption that the public will benefit by its existence." Such a conception, however weakly held, profoundly modifies the position of those in responsible positions within the corporation.

Again, the corporation, though of voluntary formation is of compulsory continuance. Neither neglect to appoint officers, nor insolvency, works

dissolution till the law is content.  Theoretically
the company is eternal.  And this, perhaps more
than any other single feature, is reflected in the
task of management.  For it must so devise its
policies and its acts that they work not for today
only nor for this generation, but for tomorrow and
the generations that come after.

A further characteristic of the corporation is
autonomy.  Within the limits set by the law it is
a self-governing community.  Its responsibility for
the acts of its servants is absolute.  Though its
control of its managers is less immediate and pervasive than is the case with a private business, the
effects of their discretion or indiscretion are none
the less its passport to triumph or to decay.  The
responsibility of the managers to the owners is both
freer from interference and postulates a higher
degree of trustworthiness.

Lastly the corporation implies compulsory
unity of action.  However much the individuals
in any industrial unit may differ among each other,
they stand to the world as one.  And this position
is a legal fact as well as a moral obligation.  The
degree of co-operation required of the company
differs in kind from that enforced by the will of
the individual owner.

These conceptions underlying the legal form
of the Joint Stock Company, more than any other
single cause, necessitate a restatement of our ideas
about management.  They may appear theoretical.
In ordinary practice the Limited Liability Company is very frequently developed from a private

business ; in consequence the spirit and management of the concern remain substantially the same as they were under private ownership.

The ideas expressed seem novel to many who have been for years the servants of Joint Stock concerns. It is just this discrepancy between the spirit underlying the form and the uses to which that form is put, the fact that these ideas do seem like theory, that constitutes the most damaging arraignment of our methods of management. Deliberate fraud in the use of the Company form is comparatively rare. Persons who, in good faith and with the best intentions in the world, neglect the health of the body to which they belong, through sheer ignorance of its essential nature, are common. The service of a company profoundly affects the relationship of any manager to his superiors, to his colleagues and to his subordinates in the enterprise.

The relationships between the industrial unit and the groups surrounding it affect the task of the manager in more obvious ways. He must be alert to the scope and implications alike of state regulation and of local by-laws. His acts must be considered, not only as they affect his isolated business, but in their interactions on all who are members of associations of traders or manufacturers to which he belongs. There is the direct effect of trade union action ; there is the influence of wider ideals and more definite aspirations on the part of the rank and file. At every point they touch on his attitude to subordinates. He can afford to ignore neither the immediate grievance nor the more distant stirrings of the social conscience. No enterprise can remain local. Its trading activities may be confined to a definite area. But things which are done at Geneva or Westminster stir it profoundly, though it may little know the source of the storm. The manager must take a wider vision, have his finger on the pulse of a larger area than the village or the borough.

The last development mentioned was the variety of assistant factors which have been developed by modern science as coadjutants to the task of production. These chiefly affect the task of management in the direction of a need for knowledge. A good manager need not necessarily be a first-class cost accountant, or chemist, or engineer, or electrician, or statistician or experimental psychologist. But whatever his position in industry, he cannot perform his task of controlling and co-operating with others unless he has a sufficient knowledge of each and all of these sciences to be able to make fruitful use of their results and to appreciate the point of view of the expert in various fields.

## II

"In its essence, scientific management involves a complete mental revolution on the part of the working man engaged in any particular establishment or industry—a complete mental revolution on the part of these men as to their duties toward their work, toward their fellow men and toward their employers. And it involves the equally complete mental revolution on the part of those on the management's side—the foreman, the superintendent, the owner of the business, the board of directors—a complete mental revolution on their part as to their duties toward their fellow workers in the management, toward their workmen, and toward all of their daily problems. . . .

"Scientific management cannot be said to exist, then, in any establishment until after this change has taken place in the mental attitude of both the management and the men, both as to their duty to co-operate in producing the largest possible surplus and as to the necessity for substituting exact scientific knowledge for opinions or the old rule of thumb or individual knowledge."—F. W. TAYLOR, *Hearings before Special Committee of the House of Representatives to Investigate the Taylor and other Systems of Shop Management.*

## CHAPTER II

THE developments in industrial structure outlined in the last chapter definitely pose a question : " On the face of it, is it likely that the methods
of management which sufficed in the earlier phases
of the factory era will pass currency to-day ? "
To that question there is only one answer. What,
then, are the new methods of management which
must be developed ? To quote from a recent
writer :

" It is not, of course, possible to describe in so many
words in what the modern business spirit consists. It is
not a matter that can be either stated or learned. It
must be absorbed gradually from a study of modern
methods and inferred from the principles that serve to
guide those methods. . . . When a man has completed
his medical education, he has either assimilated the spirit
of the profession or he has not. It is the same with
modern business."

It is noticeable that this sentence deals with the
question from the point of view of *learning* management *as a profession*. Perhaps the fundamental distinction between the older and newer methods of
management can be most easily understood from
this angle. Much of our knowledge of the way in

which people learn has been derived from experiments made by psychologists on animals.

With animals learning is essentially a matter of trial and error, and the gradual formation of a habit. Much human learning is also a matter of trial and error. But a comparison of the number of errors made by a rat, a child, and an adult in successive attempts to learn the way through a simple maze, shows that the adult has a very clear advantage over the child and still more over the rat, particularly at the start. This advantage is due to better understanding of the situation at the outset, more plan, and less tendency to go off at a tangent.

An adult faced with a mechanical puzzle for the first time uses trial and error. But at some later attempt he will suddenly get an " insight " into the working of the thing. He will grasp some relationship or principle which had previously eluded him. His solutions will become rapid and certain. This insight is based upon observation. It has to be followed by manipulation in order to give practical mastery. But manipulation without insight means slow learning, and often yields no principle that can be carried over into another situation. Animals show little sign of this observation or of the consequent analysis. Thus man learns by doing impulsively in some instances, by rational analysis in others. Much management method in the immediate past and even today is of the trial and error variety for which we must substitute rational analysis.

Methods of looking for recruits or of training new-comers emphasise this attitude to the learning process. What is stressed is not knowledge or understanding of principles, but experience. A new traveller is engaged, thrown a bag of samples, assigned a ground, and sent out to gain " experience ". A degree better, he is given a few weeks with an older hand. That brings in imitation. But imitation is still an elementary process. It is observation followed by trial and error. It is not learning in the higher sense at all. It has no trace of that analysis of the process which gives insight into principles and the conditions of future success.

Management *as a profession*? What is the difference between a professional man and a business man as the terms are at present understood ? The word profession has been defined as " a vocation involving relations to the affairs of others of such nature as to require for its proper conduct an equipment of learning or skill or both, and to warrant the community in making restrictions in respect of its exercise ". Another writer refers to " The intrinsic, as apart from the economic, interest in . . . the work " as the distinguishing mark of the professional attitude. " The most important reward is the extent to which the service is appreciated by those best competent to judge it, by those who practise the same profession."

The business man defines the breach which still separates him from the professional attitude when he declares that " He is not in business for his health." Business has just as much intrinsic interest as any other profession, a great deal more than most. But unlike the professions it does not acknowledge it. The other and higher reward is lacking in business—" the extent to which the service is appreciated by those best competent to judge it, by those who practise the same profession ". A leading K.C. will earn enormous fees, but to many the approval of fellow barristers is a higher prize and one more keenly sought. There is no reason whatever why the same should not be true of those whose occupation in life is management. But secrecy and individualism die hard. Looking round on the extraordinary self-segregation of the older form of manager, one is reminded of Lord Dundreary on proverbs. He could not imagine " that any bird could be such a silly ass as to get into a corner and flock by itself ".

What is it that the would-be manager must learn ? Is there a science of management ?

Now if the word " science " means anything it means a body of codified knowledge which satisfies those criteria of truth which the established sciences have taught us to appreciate. And the first of those criteria is that a fact if it is to be regarded as scientific must be capable of repeated proof. But the very great majority of the facts with which management in modern industry has to deal are connected with human beings, and the most important aspects of adult human beings are their mentality and temperament. The most distinguished British psychologist of the last fifty years, the late Mr. W. H. R. Rivers, says on this point :

" The science which deals with mind in its individual aspect, and still more that which attempts to deal with the collective aspect, is so much less advanced that it can hardly as yet claim to provide an answer to any of the more concrete questions which the sociologist or the statesman may wish to put to it. We cannot claim more than that psychology has reached certain general principles which will help the politician, the social reformer, or the teacher."

On the other hand management *can* use the scientific temper and the scientific method.

Take a simple problem—a process has gone wrong. What is the primary consideration, to get that process right for the moment or to make sure that it does not go wrong in the future ? In the first case a series of arbitrary experiments may lead to the right procedure. In the second case it is necessary to analyse the process into its elements, to consider step by step the procedure by which the first successful result was reached, to judge in each case the exact influence of the material employed, and so to come to an understanding of the conditions of success.

Suppose that a girl's output has fallen off. Is the immediate conclusion that she is a lazy little rascal, and, in the words of a manager of the old school, " tha' darned little slut, tha' kin tak' tha' jacket and 'op it " ? Or are there various possible causes that may have led her to drop behind her average, that she may have something wrong with her health, a point for the works doctor to determine, that she may have trouble at home and the welfare supervisor will be able to help, that the machine is out of gear and the aid of the engineering department is needed, that she is in an unsuitable job and that monotony has made her stale, a question for the psychologist? In each case the former method is the quicker and the easier. But it is not the method of men with the scientific temper, and it does not win success in the long run.

The great prison reformer Howard, in dealing with one of the many Committees which endeavoured to bring order into this department of our national life took a new line :

" Instead of sensational denunciation of oppression and cruelty, disease and promiscuity, Howard laid before the Committee a detailed statement with regard to each prison that he had visited, of the exact fees taken by the gaolers, the cubic contents, window space or depth below ground of each apartment, the number, sex, age, and grade of the prisoners confined together or apart, the exact kinds of chain or irons used, the amount and quality of food (or the absence of food) of the prisoners, and the state of the sewers and the water supply."

The truth and the importance of his allegations were established. That is an excellent example of the scientific method.

What is the contrast between scientific method and the older systems of management? It is the substitution, as far and to the full extreme which our knowledge allows, of an analysis and a basis of fact for opinion.

Much of the success of management consists in the avoidance of strife and friction of one kind and another. Industry is the task of meeting the material needs of mankind. That task has been infinitely sub-divided, which carries with it an obvious corollary. Since each individual contributes only a minute fraction to the whole of any industrial achievement, men must be induced to co-operate, to work together, and to dovetail into organisations, if any achievement is to be registered at all. At long last, the supervision and arrangement of this dovetailing, the labour of keeping men co-operating, is *the* task of management. Its challenge and difficulty lie in the following fact. Each single unit of any aggregate of human beings is equipped with certain definite and basic instincts, not to mention a much more complicated endowment of habits and customs, prejudices and ways of looking at things. He has an instinct of self-preservation, which is both individual and social, a parental instinct, an instinct of self-assertiveness or self-aggression, and an instinct of self-submission ; and pugnacity, curiosity, sex, play, workmanship all supply further underlying " drives " which help to determine individual conduct. His endowment of habits and customs, environment and the details of individual experience, interplay with these more basic tendencies. And the total result is that amazingly various mixture of sentiments and apprehensions, aspirations, and motives, the singular of which we call the character or temperament of a man, and the plural of which is " human nature ".

That is to say, management has two aspects, the mechanic and the dynamic. It has to build the machinery of co-operation, with all its cogs, and gears, transmissions, and countershaftings— banking, currency, shipping, the adjustment of processes in this factory or in that, card files, correspondence systems, every detail and turn of the technique of industry, finance, and commerce. But also it is concerned with the power behind the machinery, the wills of the individual men and women who co-operate in the task, which are the steam or the electricity which make the machine go at all.

And it is suggested that of these two aspects the issue of the power or drive is of infinitely greater importance than the other. Even an old-fashioned machine will run, and get some work done, although with a good deal of friction and waste of power. But if the power is cut off, the most modern and skilful product of engineering stands idle, so much waste iron and steel, system without spirit.

There is still a great deal of misunderstanding about science, much of it due to bad teaching. Some regard it as irreligious ; others as concerned only with details. Men say that Science is hard, inhuman, and to the young and warm-hearted and generous positively intolerable. But all the dogmas and philosophies, the patriotisms and the passions, which men have created for their use, are to be judged, much like anything else, by their results. If science is hard and inhuman, romanticism, sentimentalism, and ill-founded philosophies are harder still ; while the way of progress lies not in half-knowledge, gained easily and applied in the large, but rather in the painful and detailed winning of this fact and that, the accumulation of a real understanding of the laws and causes which rule the world.

That at least is the wider conception underlying the scientific idea.

The curious feature of the industrial situation today is this. On the mechanical side of production, on the application of the resources of nature to the production of material goods, the scientific attitude is largely supreme. But on the much more important human side of management, the task of inducing men to co-operate, the conception of scientific method is often ignored. When a machine is performing a particular process, it is realised immediately that it works according to law. If it is going badly, engineers take it to pieces and examine each separate part. Bearings are gauged, oil examined, perhaps analysed. The material is sent to the laboratory to be re-tested. In short, it is recognised that, if the machine won't work, either the principles on which it is put together are unsound or one of the essential rules underlying its operation is being neglected.

No amount of personal enthusiasm, neither kicking the machine nor abusing it, neither prayers nor tears, will make that machine function properly, unless and until those laws are understood and observed. At long last, if all other methods fail, there is a treatise on its mechanics, or more ordinarily an expert is called in to advise how to put things right. At the very least, however irritating, the affair is not regarded as a personal issue between some individual and the machine.

This attitude does not always carry over to those functions of management which have to do with similar inorganic matter, or to what has been called earlier the mechanic function of management. Take the various systems on which the smooth working of an industrial organisation depend, the systems which deal with goods, and routing, and costing, the supply of raw material and so on. In how many cases are matters left to individual judgment, which are accurately and quantitatively measurable ? The ordinary gearing of an industrial organisation on its mechanical side is as accurately determinable, as bound by the law of cause and effect, as the operation of any other piece of mechanism.

But it is in its central dynamic function, that of dealing with men and women, of inducing them to co-operate, that management is most often unscientific. Everyone is accustomed to the idea that physical efficiency is a matter of law ; at least, when the physical machine breaks down, a human consulting engineer, called a doctor, is usually called in and his advice is sometimes taken. Preventive medicine is even more effective than curative medicine. But there somehow the process stops.

Consider the field which the application of physiology to industrial processes is opening up.

Almost every industrial process involves certain muscular activities ; almost every individual has a slightly varying muscular system. Has any real attempt been made either to study the processes in various industries in accordance with the general laws of muscular health and efficiency, or to adapt the work to the individual in accordance with his requirements in this respect? A few tentative experiments are being made on the rather obvious fact that a chair suitable for the work of a girl 5 feet high is not an encouraging muscular environment for a girl 5 feet 10 inches high. But uniform benches are still a feature of most factories, and a left-handed man is put to work at a machine which was designed for a right-handed man without a thought. There are rows of machines in many factories which appear to have been designed for the purpose of ensuring that the worker does the maximum of stopping and stretching, and spends the longest possible portion of the working hours in thoroughly unhealthy positions. Meanwhile, the machine next door is proof positive that such an arrangement was not in the least necessary to the efficient working of the process.

Another matter is ventilation. To quote from a recent enquiry :

" Physiological research has shown that the *physical* rather than the *chemical* properties of the air are responsible for the general feeling of good health and vigour which results from exposure to a bracing wind. Such a wind exerts a strong cooling action on the skin, and stimulates the nerve endings. A cold skin encourages exercise to maintain warmth, stimulates deeper breathing, increases the circulation of the blood, promotes more rapid and complete digestion, and so produces a generally improved state of health."

Obviously, therefore, the temperature of a room, as ascertained by an ordinary mercury thermometer, is not a good indication as to the healthfulness of the system of ventilation. It is even more important that the air should be moving, and should give a cooling speed adapted to the process in question. Instruments have been perfected for testing this cooling speed. It is undoubtedly possible to determine optimum rates of cooling for any given process and any given room, rates which should contribute vitally to the general health of the worker.

So much for men's bodies, their physical constitution. What of their minds? Here again, there is a certain amount of popular recognition of the therapeutic value of psychological ideas. Men accept the conception that there are certain processes which function in the mind below the threshold of consciousness. It is recognised that failure in the organisation of the sub-conscious processes leads to one or other of such processes exercising an excessive " drive " over conduct, frequently in a direction opposite to the individual's traditional mental and moral habit. From this conflict arise hysteria, nervous breakdown, and other mental abnormalities. The success in treating shell-shock constructively on purely mental lines, by analysing and rationalising to the sufferer the sources of conflict which had produced his disorder, and showing him, as it were, how to rearrange the cogs, has definitely established psychological treatment as a branch of medical practice.

But there is a great unwillingness to carry over the thought which we apply to cure, into ordinary life for purposes of prevention. Take the individual and his equipment of instincts. Surely psychology can help industry here. Changing a man over from one machine to another, for some very good reason, sometimes arouses a suspicion and cold fury which astonishes the management. It is only a sense of proprietorship, compounded of the self-assertive and parental instincts. His very language betrays the fact. He talks about " my machine ". It isn't his, but his employer's. Nevertheless, he is not an unreasonable ass. He is obeying a deep-seated impulse, and if friction is to be avoided it is better to start with the reason and leave the order to change, till he has had time to let a rational process supervene and control the first prompting of that impulse.

Then there are labour turnover and industrial misfits. One man does badly at one job, then at a second, and suddenly quite well at a third, after wasting two or three years and a lot of distress into the bargain. Usually it is said that he has changed in the most amazing way. He has not changed, and it isn't amazing. Some men have one type of memory, which recognises things by their sound, or by auditory imagery, as the psychologists call it. Others remember things by painting a picture in their mind of the event they wish to remember, or by visual imagery, as it is called. One man can concentrate his attention closely on a limited field of observation, and another has a clear and comprehensive grasp of a wide field, but no power of concentration at all. Obviously, there are jobs which will suit the first man and not the second, and *vice versa*. Yet the man with wide attention is trained as a watchmaker, and the man with concentrated attention is set to drive a motor-car in traffic.

Experimental psychology has devised, and is rapidly improving, definite tests for comparing individuals in respect of various functions of the mind. The achievements of " vocational selection ", as it is called, are yet in their infancy. But a million and a quarter men of the recruits for the American army were tested by standardised methods, both for general intelligence and for specific capacities. The results of those tests were of enormous practical value in selection for promotion and in allocating men to the various technical branches of the service.

Some people have a mental constitution which is excessively sensitive to the effects of monotonous repetition work, others have not ; and the difference has no direct connection with their general level of intelligence. Some people respond well to the stimulus of a high piece-rate, or even a progressive bonus ; others are harassed by it, and develop less than their full efficiency.

No less important than individual psychology

is the question of group psychology. This study necessarily presents enormous difficulties to experimental work. If anyone tries to experiment with a revivalist meeting, an angry strike crowd, or the men who have backed the winner after a welshing bookmaker, his devotion to pure science certainly does not lack an element of self-sacrifice. But industry day by day is constantly called upon to deal with men in groups, and the distinction between their group outlook and mentality and their outlook and mentality as individuals is clearly of first-rate importance. Considerable study has been devoted to the games of London school-children when organised in groups. Other examples of directions in which enquiry is proceeding are afforded by group rhythms of various kinds, and their influence on work ; the sailors' chanty is an example.

But beyond these cases where the exact or sociological sciences have a definite contribution to make to a specific problem, every question that faces the business manager can be approached in the scientific temper. There can be applied to it the five-fold intellectual technique of definition, analysis, measurement, experiment and proof which is characterisuc of work in the exact sciences. Management is gradually developing a definite technique of its own, scientific methods and procedure for dealing with its problems. But the task is only at the beginning. It is the spirit that is of importance. The material sciences have given man a grip over the resources of the natural world undreamed of in former ages. His great problem is to place his knowledge of human factors and causes, of himself in short, on a plane which will enable him to cope with the responsibility of that amazing access of power. Is it likely that the older methods will suffice? Is it not inherently probable that the lines of thought on which he has solved his problems in material will prove the discipline which will enable him to solve his problems in men?

Forty years ago a young engineer in Detroit had a theory as to the coming of motor traction. His is the most colossal single personal industrial achievement of our time. He speaks of " those who are so perfectly void of vision that they are sometimes regarded as practical men ". Much though men may love the old traditions and the old ways, industry brooks no tarrying.

## III

"The motive power which is really going to change the external surface of civilisation, which is going to add to the material well-being of mankind, which is going to stimulate the imagination of all those who are interested in the Universe in which our lot is cast—that lies after all with science. I would rather be known as having added to our sum of knowledge of human nature than anything else I can imagine."
—A. J. BALFOUR (afterwards Lord), speaking at Leeds, 1909.

"If industry is the chief exponent of modern action, it is without question that science is the leading exponent of modern thought. What results may be expected for the human race when these two things shall work together harmoniously and intimately!"—E. D. JONES, *Industrial Leadership and Executive Ability*.

## CHAPTER III

### RESEARCH INTO MANAGEMENT

THE foundation of all scientific work is, of course, research. Yet it was only at its centenary meeting that, *for the first time*, the British Association for the Advancement of Science included in its programme of sectional meetings, concerned with progress in this or that specialised branch of scientific work, a more general section devoted to industrial co-operation.

This fact is significant as illustrating the lag in social psychology, in our powers of mental adaptation. As law always trails after public opinion, so men's attempts to understand and to control their common life are usually in terms of habits and of technical patterns which have long ceased to correspond with reality.

Excited with the material possibilities which the new techniques of machine production opened up, men did not pause to think of the intellectual processes, of the logic of thought which underlay the new knowledge or of its bearing upon their general attitudes towards each other. The existing political and economic patterns of society were taken for granted, as were the relations they imposed. Those in positions of leadership and authority merely grafted each fresh development on to the body of their current practice, without modifying that practice save in so far as was absolutely necessary to make use of this or that aspect of applied scientific work.

Even today the industrialist engages chemists or engineers, the banker hires an economist, or the advertising agent a statistician rather in the frame of mind of a man who calls in a doctor unwillingly to please his wife. Indeed, with the structure of society manifestly incapable of dealing with the consequences of an unreflecting orgy on the proceeds of technical development, many of its leaders are still muttering " never had a day's illness in my life ". The scientist is still regarded largely as a specialist, somebody contributing from without a thin stream of technical skill into the broad flood of normal business practice. When, in fact, the bones and flesh and blood, the vital principle which has made modern business practicable at all is science. Only through the intellectual processes which created the machines can men become masters of a machine environment.

This consideration points to some of the larger aims which lie before those who are interested in research into management problems. Briefly, those aims are to bring to bear both the whole volume of existing scientific knowledge and the scientific technique in solving every problem bearing upon all the legislative, planning, directing, supervising and controlling activities involved in economic operations. Nor, indeed, is the significance of management research confined to economic enterprises. Management problems press for solution wherever men and women are associated together for the pursuit of a common objective.

One of the chief results which may be anticipated from a more scientific examination of business management is a growing recognition of the essential unity of management processes, whatever the purpose to which they are applied. Such recognition and the comparisons to which it must give rise will greatly enrich men's knowledge both of the field as a whole and of the possibilities under a given set of conditions. The research worker in management has therefore little concern with the popular distinction which discriminates between organisations on the ground of the objective which they are designed to serve or of the particular form of ownership which determines their higher control.

Since the problems of management arise when men and women are associated together for a given purpose, they are necessarily human problems. It may well be asked, then, how they can be approached scientifically? It is clear that current knowledge of individual and social psychology are alike inadequate to provide a foundation of exact fact, or to predict accurately how human beings will behave under given circumstances.

What is meant by the scientific approach is best understood by comparison with the medical profession. The training which the would-be medical man has to undergo has a triple purpose. In the first place, there are a large number of sciences underlying the practice of medicine, just as certain sciences, psychology, statistics, engineering and so on, underlie industrial practice. These he is expected to understand sufficiently to appreciate the bearing of fresh developments in such sciences on the existing body of medical knowledge.

In the second place, where exact knowledge fails him, he is still expected to apply analysis, measurement and proof—the three great weapons of scientific method—to his problems. The process of diagnosis in the case of human ailments is comparable to the process by which a skilled mechanic diagnoses the fault on a stalled motor-car. To the helpless owner-driver it may seem instantaneous and miraculous. But the same procedure of analysis, test, rejection of alternative possibilities and final isolation of the effective factor always takes place, however foreshortened by experience and skill.

In the third place, he is taught the ethics of his profession. And these include an obligation to pool his experience in the common interest of his fellow-practitioners for the general advancement of medical science.

The methods of research into management correspond to these three features of medical training. There is, first of all, the enlargement of the corpus of knowledge represented by each of the sciences which underlie industrial practice. This is chiefly a matter of laboratory work in the broad sense. It is carried on by psychological institutions, research departments connected with universities, and similar bodies. It may be concerned with such questions as the clearer understanding of the phenomenon of fatigue, a refinement of statistical procedure, or an investigation of atmospheric humidity.

There is also a considerable volume of work of a similar laboratory character directed on to the immediate problems of industrial management, particularly in the United States and in Germany. Thus a research may be undertaken into the incidence of lateness in different age groups or occupations or at different seasons of the year among the personnel of a given factory or industry, or of a variety of factories or industries within a defined locality, or generally. Or, again, the subject studied may be the effectiveness of suggestion schemes for employees.

Such studies vary enormously in their scientific significance. What distinguishes them generally is the fact that they are definite attempts, conducted by disinterested theoretical workers, either to enlarge the boundaries of an existing department of science or to apply scientific methods to discover general principles governing some aspect of management. According to the nature of the problem, the methods employed are those of the exact or of the sociological sciences.

The third type of research, corresponding closely to field work by medical research workers, is found in cases where a factory calls in theoretical workers either to solve a particular problem, or, more rarely, to make a general investigation under controlled conditions into the factors affecting the output of a given group of employees. Here the objective differs slightly in that the factory is seeking information for its own immediate purposes. But there is an increasing tendency for scientific workers to insist on the integrities of their professional standing and to demand that they shall be permitted to publish, at all events after a reasonable interval, results which are of general interest.

But the opportunities and the resources at the disposal of theoretical workers are of course very much smaller than those represented by the huge mass of day-by-day management of business processes. And just as the body of medical knowledge is largely dependent on the observations and recorded experience of countless general practitioners, so the development of management principles must ultimately depend on the degree to which the great body of managers can be induced to approach their problems in a scientific spirit.

As Dr. Person, the Director of the Taylor Society, has recently pointed out, there has been a logical and progressive development in the subjects in the field of industrial management which have been submitted to scientific enquiry in the individual enterprise. The first series of phenomena investigated dealt with the efficacy of the individual workman at the workplace. They included such questions as the design of equipment, size and output of machines, the behaviour of material, skill, and methods as revealed by time

and motion studies.  But it was quickly apparent
that right solutions of these problems depended not
only on conditions at the individual workplace,
but on the organisation of the shop.  This led to
studies of the relations between facilities and classes
of skill available at the various workplaces, and
their effective co-ordination and adjustment under
varying conditions as to the kind and quantities of
work called for.  Comparisons thus instigated revealed discrepancies which called attention to questions of personnel, such as the mental and manual
aptitudes of individuals, the type of personality
required for various jobs, emotional conditions and
reactions, and group psychology.

Gradual improvement in these factors pushed
the problem back a step to the conditions determining the volume of work required, that is, the
market.  Investigation centred on quantitative and
qualitative market analysis, consumer demand,
channels of distribution, selling methods, and so on.
But enquiries in these fields could not evade the
interdependence of these subjects with the financial
structure of the enterprise.  The microscope was
turned on to costs, the market for capital, credits
and collections, prices of material, and financial
ratios.  Again, the connection with General Administration was inescapable.  Scientific method
was employed to forecast tendencies in industry
generally and in the particular industry and enterprise, to control the relative efficiency of various
departments, and to analyse organisation structure.
The researches conducted by all departments con-

tributed to the information required by general administration.[1]

There is no question whatever that those who have approached the problems of the management of individual factories in the scientific spirit have benefited enormously. Outputs, comfort in work, sales, profits, relations with employees—every aspect of their operations have gained in effectiveness. Nor is there any question that the number of those who seek to apply these methods is constantly upon the increase. Two principal difficulties retard development.

In the first place, the very volume of work that is being done and published makes it difficult for the average manager to keep pace with new developments, despite the increased specialisation of function which characterises industrial organisation. To initiate experiments without making sure that the results of similar experiments are not available is wasteful. Yet, where hundreds of factories in half a dozen countries are attempting solutions of similar problems, when there are at least 20,000 volumes in the management field, when one country alone publishes over 100 periodicals a month devoted to management questions, how can the busy manager hope to keep pace with his job? A partial solution has been found by management institutions in different countries which select among this large mass of literature, and publish

[1] Adapted from *Principles and Practice of Scientific Management*, paper presented by Dr. H. S. Person to the World Social Economic Congress, Amsterdam, 1931.

digests and notes bearing upon any development
which is really original or worthy of note. The
same function is carried out internationally by the
International Management Institute at Geneva. It
may be noted that there is at present no such
institution in Great Britain. Even where such
institutions exist, however, the problem remains a
serious one.

There are signs of a substantial improvement
in this position. In the first place, an increasing
proportion of managers are selected who have
received formal training in one or other of the
underlying sciences. This involves a greater
capacity both to read quickly and to select what is
read. This, in its turn, reflects on the quantity
and quality of the literature published. There is
already observable in the United States and in
Germany an impatience with the flood of periodical
generalisations and repetitions bearing on management, as also of the type of book written to enhance
personal prestige. In each of the fields of management there are gradually emerging recognised
authorities whose texts remain standard for their
subject for a considerable period.

The second difficulty is more serious. However scientific the management in a given factory
may be, the solutions of particular problems
remain isolated. Competition may have increased
efficiency by encouraging the survival of the fittest,
it has certainly slowed development in so far as it
has discouraged the direct measurement one against
the other of the performances of individuals dis-

charging identical functions. That is to say, the test of effectiveness has been limited to the broad issue of whether one enterprise makes a profit as against another enterprise. But this broad test is not sufficiently refined. It does not provide a method of measurement which throws light on the details of comparative performance. And it is by such refined and detailed comparisons that real progress in knowledge is achieved.

Two movements may be noted as tending towards a resolution of this obstacle. In a number of countries groups have been formed of non-competing, and in some cases of competing, enterprises, pledged to organised co-operation in the examination of their management problems. The stimulating effect on managers of comparing experience systematically, even with eight or nine others engaged on like tasks, has been emphasised by all who have made a real effort to collaborate in such work. Incidentally, substantial financial economies have been effected as the direct result of information obtained through the groups. Taylor, the founder of Scientific Management, always insisted that experiments—even when spread over a period of years—should yield an interim dividend, be made to pay as they developed. There are now more than fifty of such groups in nine countries, and three international groups.

In the second place, there is the growing use of management ratios. A management ratio may be defined as the relation established between the effort expended in any activity and some defined and comparable base. The National Association of Office Managers in the U.S.A. has recently initiated a campaign to obtain management ratios from several hundred enterprises bearing on every type of clerical operation. The results already obtained have been sufficiently arresting. The cost of pencils per clerk per year revealed differences between undertakings amounting to staggering percentages. The cost per letter despatched of an average length of 20 lines was equally revealing. And so on through the whole gamut of operations at present investigated.

The third element emphasised in medical training was instruction in the ethics of the profession, including complete frankness as to methods for the general advancement of medical knowledge. Here the position with regard to management research is very mixed. Certain functions have been recognised as possessing a definite professional standing. Engineering and accountancy and law are in this position in Great Britain : sales management and advertising are on the way there. But the competitive traditions of business have prevented the full growth of a vivid sense of the existence of a general technique which belongs not to the individual but to the profession as a whole and to contribute to which is the duty and pride of every serious member of that profession.

This spirit, while not wholly lacking, is less active and fruitful than it might be. There are large areas of business management which are at present untouched by it. The growth of professional organisation among these elements and the awakening of a greater sense of obligation to enlarge the boundaries of professional knowledge, are among the directions from which research in management may be most powerfully reinforced in the near future.

Management Research has thus three main lines of development. There is, first of all, what has been called laboratory research, directed either towards extension of one of the sciences underlying management or towards their application to a specific management problem. It is usually carried out by specialist workers. There is, secondly, research within the factory carried on by the managing staff in the search for higher efficiency through scientific method. Co-operation in this work may be intensive through management groups or extensive by contributions to and comparisons drawn from management ratios. Thirdly, there is research by the same groups carried on outside the factory through their association in professional institutions.

Up to this point management research has been discussed with reference to the problems of management as they exist today in relation to the individual enterprise. But bitter experience has emphasised the fact that the process of expansion cannot stop at the factory boundary. Civilisation is doomed to revolutionary change, if not to social chaos, unless it can achieve methods of organisation in the near future which will give control of the forces released by a rapidly mechanised economy.

Already experiments have been undertaken here and there, as in Germany under the title of Rationalisation. That movement towards a higher integration of industrial elements on a national scale, despite inevitable mistakes, had this result, that in the first ten months of 1930 Germany's five great export industries lost only 7 per cent. in value and less in volume as compared with 1929. It would be a mistake to allow subsequent economic difficulties due to political and financial causes to obscure the significance of such figures.

Little is known of the principles which should govern the administration of the large-scale combinations of previously independent units so increasingly characteristic of modern business. The popular view usually identifies some " organising genius " as their real architect and creator. Even genius cannot create principles of organisations ; it can only apply them. And if these principles can be discovered, adequately identified, and properly taught, qualities far short of genius will be adequate for their effective application. The study of large-scale business administration and of the special problems which it presents is one of the most urgent problems which faces management research.

A similar problem is presented by looser arrangements, such as cartels. Here economic reasons are usually assigned for failure. But administrative ineptitude may be equally responsible. A scientific study of cartel management awaits the combination of available resources and a suitable research worker.

Beyond combinations and cartels lie the problems of industries considered as a whole. Such problems include standardisation, simplification, regulation of productive capacity, fundamental research, and so on. The construction and maintenance of policies on such questions is a matter for management research. It may be noted that in the United States, where anti-trust legislation on the one hand and absence of labour organisation on the other prevent the dissipation of a large percentage of their resources, either in maintaining price-rings or in fighting labour, certain of the best Trade Associations have been making noteworthy experiments in this field. But the subject is only in its infancy.

At a further stage still come the questions involved in the management of national economies and of the world economy. Not even the most conservative of financiers can pretend that the management of the world's currency and financial machinery in the last ten years has been a model of conspicuous efficiency. Again, most industries and most countries are complaining about over-production. But there is not a single European state which publishes adequate figures bearing on the facts as to domestic consumption and distribution. There is constant criticism not only of industrial and business leadership, but of governmental administration. If, for a moment, the countries concerned could call a truce in the wholly theoretical controversy as to whether enterprises owned by the community can or cannot be efficient in principle, and apply management research to such organisms with a view to making them efficient, they would attain real economies.

The present position will not brook much further delay. On every side traditional thinking combines with vested interests of all kinds to oppose a scientific reorganisation of the world economy. Fundamentally, as with all great issues, the problem is a simple one. Science has issued in power production. Power production has enormously increased man's capacity to supply the material requirements on which human life depends. The world economy is technically in a better position than it has ever been before to fulfil the fundamental function of any economic system—to raise progressively the standard of living of those dependent on it.

Were it possible to agree as between the nations that the purpose of all economy, the objective to which every proposal should be referred, was a higher standard of life for the world community, there is no inherent impossibility in applying the conceptions and technique of management research to every aspect and level of economic activity. Until it is done, until modern business is conducted in conformity with the principles which created it, the present confusion will not only continue, but grow inevitably worse. From the management standpoint science is concerned with one central question, how, in the light of an objective consideration of the facts, the economic system may be organised at every level, from the worker at the bench to the last details of international exchange, so as most effectively to fulfil its defined function ?

There is no alternative. At the moment the facts of the system of trade and industry by which the peoples live are world-wide and interdependent. The conceptions on which it is conducted are scarcely adequate to the successful management of a series of village shops. Continuance in these conceptions will lead, sooner rather than later, to widespread social disorder. And when that price in blood and starvation has been paid, mankind will be much where it is today, poorer, less certain, but still seeking for that "law of the situation" which humanity must obey or perish.

The roots of wealth are planted in exact knowledge. Only by an extension of that knowledge can we secure that from wealth springs also welfare.

# PART TWO

## ORGANISATION

### IV

" Technique implies an art, and the technique of organization, like every art, must have its principles. To prove the reality of these principles it is only necessary to observe the same general forms always appearing in every kind of associated human effort. When we observe that the same forms, with their characteristic relationships, which are omnipresent in secular government, are likewise universal in church organization, ancient and modern, and that modern industrial organization, in all its variants, simply repeats the same old story, we realize that we are face to face with something fundamental in all organized human effort."—JAMES D. MOONEY and ALAN C. REILEY, *Onward Industry*.

" As long as armies were small . . . the plan determined upon by the General in command usually contained the details of execution. But few directions were therefore necessary to secure, in the way that was intended, the quartering, concentration, and general advance . . . of an army. . . . But this state of affairs no longer exists. The enormous numerical strength of modern armies, and the way they must be organized to meet the constantly changing requirements of war, render an immense amount of detail necessary in carrying out military operations. . . . Thus, the higher leaders and commanders necessarily require the permanent support of specially selected and trained officers."—VON SCHELLENDORFF, *The Duties of the General Staff*. (Quoted by the late Lord Haldane in the Memorandum accompanying the Special Army Order constituting a General Staff for the British Army, September 12th, 1906.)

## CHAPTER IV

### THE PURE THEORY OF ORGANISATION

THE word "organisation" is used in a number of different senses. In the first place it is used as a substantive connoting a group of people united for a purpose. In this sense an organisation comes into being wherever such a grouping takes place. The larger the group, the more complex will be its character. But however small the group may be and however rudimentary its arrangements for collaboration, there an organisation exists. It is not something which is a matter of volition, which can be accepted or rejected at will. It comes into existence automatically, when a common object is pursued by a group of co-workers.

In addition to its use as a general substantive to describe the group as a whole, "organisation" is also frequently employed specifically to describe the body of arrangements which exist for securing collaboration between the members of the group; in this sense it connotes the system or methods established. This use of the term may be either concrete, referring to a particular instance, or abstract, implying system or method in general. These two uses may be illustrated by such a sen-

tence as " X Bros. & Co. have a fine organisation :
it was installed by Mr. Y who has a keen sense of
organisation." In the second place the word is
frequently used in place of the participle, implying the process of organising, for instance in such
a sentence as " organisation, which is a task calling
for close analysis ".

This variety of uses of the same term is itself
indicative of a certain confusion as to the exact
significance of the object or process which it
describes. In this chapter the word will be used
in the sense of a process. It may be defined as
" *dividing up all the activities which are necessary to any
purpose and arranging them in groups which are assigned
to individuals* ".

Admitting that the process of organisation
necessarily involves selection among persons, it is
clear that its theoretical consideration cannot be
reduced to terms of final validity from the scientific standpoint.

The fact, however, that a particular science
cannot be comprehensive in its results in no way
implies that the study of the subject concerned
from a theoretical standpoint may not be of great
utility for practical life, provided that the underlying assumptions on which the theoretical structure is built up are not too far removed from the
probabilities indicated by general experience of
human behaviour. There is no ground for an
assumption that in matters where organisation is
concerned there is likely to prove to be a smaller
common factor of behaviour than in questions

where economic activity is under consideration. Indeed, the reverse is the case. For economics makes an assumption as to motive, admittedly one of the aspects of human conduct least susceptible to exact measurement. But in studying administration, at all events in much of the earlier work of developing a theory of the subject, the question of motive can be ignored. It is sufficient to assume that motive exists in some form, whether that form be the enthusiasm of the seeker after pure knowledge or the threat of the firing squad.

Economic science has been gravely handicapped by the fact that business transactions, under the influence of a competitive system, have been subjected to a traditional secrecy, which, whether justifiable or not in any given case, has undoubtedly retarded to a large degree the application of inductive methods. On the other hand the factual basis for administrative studies is to some extent in the history books, and to a larger degree still has been a subject of that legitimate self-esteem which makes memoirs and diaries such a mine of information. The main obstacles to such a study are to be found elsewhere, and mainly in the assumption that success in the task of organisation is a personal matter, the emanation of a certain individual competence rather than the result of the application of principles. A further prejudice which has delayed any serious attempt to undertake a complete survey of the subject from the theoretical standpoint is the conviction that a difference in the purpose or object for which organisation is undertaken will, in itself, be the predominant factor in determining the form which that organisation will take. That is to say that there is no body of experience of administrative efforts directed to one purpose which has any validity for the study of organisation when the purpose is different.

At the present juncture when the forms of business undertakings are being subjected to very rapid change under the influence of technological considerations this latter issue is of very wide significance. With regard to the organisation of individual businesses it has for a long period prevented the mobilisation of the large amount of factual material bearing on the problems involved. Business men have hesitated from competitive considerations to discuss the details of their own undertakings with those in the same trade or industry. On the other hand they have tended to assume that the experience of those in other lines of trade cannot be of practical utility in solving their own problems. The anatomist has welcomed the guinea-pig and the rat for the light they can throw on " Homo Sapiens ". But the butcher and the baker have been doubtful whether the candlestick-maker could throw light on anything at all.

• Again, where knowledge of others' methods and problems exists in the business world it is almost entirely individual and accidental. The very large business aggregations which are increasingly characteristic of our times are creating problems of administration of a size and quality not previously contemplated by industrial leaders.

This tendency prevents them from benefiting by the experience of other forms of large-scale organisation, such as governments, churches, or armies. There has been little deliberate study of the material available. And, with rare exceptions, business men who are responsible for the control of these large amalgamations have not displayed any consciousness of the need for or possibilities of systematic investigation.

There is thus a strong case for an attempt to build a pure theory of organisation and to direct that attempt particularly towards business organisation. Such an attempt must in the long run be inductive. It must be based on a widespread study of past and existing enterprises both in business and in other walks of life. From such an objective study will be collated the factual material on which guiding principles can be based. While such principles will admittedly not enable fools to manage great businesses, they will provide a framework within which both genius and intelligent leadership of the second grade can function with greater effect, and changes can take place in the controlling personnel with fewer risks than is the case today.

Such a study will be based on certain assumptions. Alongside the " economic man " of the nineteenth century must be placed an " administrative man " of the twentieth. There seems no reason to suppose that he will prove a less useful intellectual conception than his predecessor. The weakness of the conception of the " economic man " has been its static character :

" In all the received formulations of economic theory, . . . the human material with which the enquiry is concerned is conceived in hedonistic terms ; that is to say in terms of a passive and substantially inert and immutably given human nature. . . . The hedonistic conception of man is that of a lightning calculator of pleasures and pains, who oscillates like a homogeneous globule of desire of happiness under the impulse of stimuli that shift him about the area, but leave him intact. . . . Spiritually the hedonistic man is not a prime mover. He is not the seat of a process of living, except in the sense that he is subject to a series of permutations enforced upon him by circumstances external and alien to him." [1]

It is this feature of economic theory which has placed economics out of touch with modern developments in the biological, psychological and sociological sciences—sciences which are fundamentally evolutionary in their point of view :

" The economists have accepted the hedonistic preconceptions concerning human nature and human action. . . . Under hedonism the economic interest is not conceived in terms of action. It is therefore not readily apprehended or appreciated in terms of a cumulative growth of habits of thought, and does not provoke, even if it did lend itself to, treatment by the evolutionary method." [2]

In so far, however, as the hedonistic idea has postulated a certain uniformity in human reaction to circumstances, a pattern which will yield similar

[1] Thorstein Veblen on " Economics and Evolution " in *The Place of Science in Modern Civilisation*, p. 73, New York, 1919.
[2] *Ibid.*, p. 78.

results as the consequence of similar causes or conditions, it has assisted understanding of economic processes and the establishment of principles as a guide to action.  Nor is there any reason why a science of organisation should fall into the same error of inertia.  Indeed, since it must necessarily derive much of its material from historical sources, the fact of process, of growth and change, even in human nature, will be constantly before it.

Since by definition organisation arises out of the activities necessary for a purpose, organisation must depend on that purpose.  *Organisation is the expression of policy either stated or implied.*  This is invariably so, and yet is rarely recognised to be so.  It is so far the exception to find cases where even the general policy of a business has been definitely formulated in writing.  A purpose exists, of course, more defined than the mere vague objective of " making money ".  But this purpose frequently gets no farther than the brain of the man in charge, where it remains, more or less definite, more or less formulated, more or less consistent, according to the quality of its environment.  Lack of any definite underlying policy, failure to relate the various activities undertaken to such a policy, are frequent causes of deplorable waste in organisation.

Again, by definition organisation consists in dividing up the activities necessary to a given purpose.  From this the second principle of organisation flows automatically.  *The first essential in the process of organisation is a complete list of the activities necessary to fulfil the policy laid down.* There are certain activities which are essential to all forms of co-ordinated human effort whatever its purpose —the activities connected with the recruitment, supervision, and maintenance of the requisite staff, for instance. Generally speaking, undertakings belonging to the same general group will call for a similar range of activities. The activities or functions called for by all business enterprises are similar, with one or two exceptions determined by the special character of the business contemplated.

The necessity for each and all such activities is inherent in the purpose for which the undertaking has been set up and is independent of individual choice or of the size of the undertaking. Theoretically the one-man business must provide for all the various specialised activities of the mammoth concern—by a division and arrangement of the time and effort of the individual involved. The mammoth concern divides them up amongst a hierarchy of officials and specialists with their subordinates. But the activities are essentially the same. From this flows the third principle of organisation—*the activities necessary to the achievement of the same or similar purposes are constant, irrespective of the size of the undertaking.*

Where however a number of individuals are associated in an undertaking, activities arise in connection with the co-ordination, direction and control of the work of others. There is a grouping of activities in two senses—into kinds and into grades of authority and responsibility.

The main considerations underlying the necessity for grouping into grades are two-fold. In the first place, though instances may arise where groups of men work harmoniously and effectively without any formal arrangement for the exercise of authority and responsibility, it will usually be discovered either that they are informally exercised by some one personality or that their place is effectively taken by custom supported by religious or other traditional sanctions. For practical purposes, and under any conditions conceivable in modern business, leadership must exist and provision be made for these activities.

In the second place, where the effective execution of these functions is under consideration, there is a clear limit to the number of subordinates who can be controlled directly by one man. Sir Ian Hamilton in a discussion of this point has declared categorically " the human brain cannot directly control more than five or six other brains ".[1] Circumstances may occur which call for a modification of this dictum. Where the individuals supervised have no relationship with each other or perform substantially uniform functions, some increase in the numbers supervised is possible. But, where those supervised have of necessity intimate working relationships, the complexity of the personal combinations which have to be taken into consideration on any issue places a strict limit on the numbers which can be controlled effectively.

From these considerations follow two further

[1] Sir Ian Hamilton, *The Soul and Body of an Army.*

principles. *Where a number of persons are associated for a common purpose it is necessary to provide for the co-ordination, direction, and control of their activities. The grouping of the activities involved in an undertaking is therefore two-fold. There is a division into different kinds of activity and there is a division into different levels of activity.*

*Since one human brain cannot directly control more than a limited number of other brains the number of groups on any one level into which any complex activity is divided for purposes of administration must not exceed this number. At the same time the number of levels of activity must be sufficient to enable this principle to be observed throughout the undertaking.*

The grouping of tasks into kinds usually follows one of four main methods :

(1) The total task is sub-divided by process, e.g. in a motor factory one man is placed in charge of the foundry, another of rough finishing, another of the machine shop, another of the assembly line, another of the testing shop, etc., etc. This is usually known as the " serial " form of organisation.

(2) The total task is subdivided by geographical areas, as when one man is placed in charge of works in Glasgow and another in charge of works in London, or Great Britain is divided into four main sales areas.

(3) The total task is subdivided by objects, as when one man is placed in charge of the production of all envelopes and another man in charge of the production of all note-

paper in a paper factory. This and the preceding type are usually described as the " unitary " form of organisation.

(4) The total task is subdivided by subjects. That is to say, one man is placed in charge of all questions of a personal nature, and another in charge of questions of accountancy, etc., etc. This is usually known as the " functional " form of organisation.

Of recent years there has been a great increase in the use of the " functional " method of dividing tasks. This is largely due to the increase of scientific knowledge. An individual charged with the control of a unit, area, or process must be responsible for decisions on all the matters which arise in connection with that part of the organisation and the personnel employed in it. But he cannot be equally an expert in every aspect of its work and management. On the other hand, the direction requires assurance that each special aspect of the management is carried out in the light of the fullest scientific knowledge available and with maximum efficiency. Thus experts are placed in charge of different kinds of work, wherever they occur in the enterprise.

Business is being forced more and more towards functionalisation. It is many years since accountancy was carved out of the mass of general management into a special profession, with standards and a technique of its own. The embryo has since propagated by subdivision into cost accountancy, actuarial technique, and its newest development—the various specialised forms of statistical practice. Engineers and chemists have always had their own peculiar skills. Sales Managers and Advertising Men are following rapidly in their footsteps. Before very many decades have passed every aspect of business management will be thus specialised and professionalised.

This development is however causing very great difficulties in organisation, due to the fact that it appears to run counter to the principles which should govern the subdivision of authority and responsibility into levels. Co-ordination has been described as *the* principle of organisation. But it is essential to the conception of co-ordination that " *the supreme co-ordinating authority must rest somewhere and in some form in every organisation* ". It is equally essential that " *there should be a process, formal in character, through which this co-ordinating authority operates from the top throughout the entire structure of the organised body* ". This is sometimes called " the scalar process " or " line " control.

In any large organisation, however, if the chief delegates his authority to five people on a functional basis, that five-fold division will run right through into every corner of the organisation. So, for instance, a foreman in a branch factory in Aberdeen will really be working under the authority of five functional chiefs in London. In such conditions real co-ordination is impossible. There must be co-ordinating authority at lower levels of the chain of responsibility. If, however, the chief has two or three individuals to whom he delegates

F

authority and responsibility on a serial or unitary basis, he can only delegate authority to one or two functional experts. And this implies insufficient specialisation. If the specialisation takes place at lower levels, the supervision of specialist functions will either be of inferior quality or have insufficient authority, or there will be the same crossing of functional authorities and lack of co-ordination at yet lower levels of the chain of responsibility.

Attempts so far made to solve this problem in industry have been in the nature of a compromise between the necessity for specialisation in control and the necessity for preserving the direct line of authority. It has been said that the specialists are " purely advisory " and all sorts of relationships have been laid down between the specialist authorities and the managers of departments on a unitary or serial basis. Great difficulty has been found in securing co-ordination. These various compromises have been described generically in industry as " the staff and line " method of organisation.

This use of the word " staff " is however a misnomer. In military life, where " staff " principles have been worked out through centuries of experience, " staff " is not applied either to those exercising authority and responsibility on a unitary basis—" the line "—or to those exercising authority and responsibility on a functional basis—specialised troops and administrative services. It has been recognised that if the " scalar process " is to be secured no chief can delegate any of his authority or responsibility except through that process. He cannot delegate for instance any part of the responsibility for the condition of the defences under the command of a Colonel of Infantry to his Chief Engineer, since the condition of the defences is part of the responsibility for holding the position which rests with the Colonel of Infantry.

Since, however, he needs specialists' work, and supervision, and authority in such matters he can only secure this by the most detailed co-ordination of specialists and line in carrying out his plans. While he cannot delegate any of his authority and responsibility, he can delegate all of the detailed work involved in the exercise of that authority and responsibility. Thus there has grown up a class of officers—the " staff ", who have no responsibility or authority personally, but who exercise their chief's authority in assisting him to carry out his responsibilities of command.

By graduations of authority and subdivision of work within the " staff " there is built up a structure by which the chief can assure himself that all the detailed consequences of any decision have been worked out, are understood, and are being carried out in correlation by everyone under his command, both specialists of all kinds and troops of the line. The authority of his line commanders is not interfered with. The orders issued by the " staff " are the chief's orders. He has only four or five people reporting to him, his principal " line " subordinates and his chief-of-staff. But through his chief-of-staff he can secure the advice of any one of a dozen specialists. It is the duty of the chief-of-staff to secure that that advice has been asked on any question affecting the functions of those specialists, and that in every action all the specialist points of view have been taken into account and the fullest possible use made of their contribution, whether advisory or executive.

The " staff " in short are not individuals who " specialise " in any one kind of work, but individuals who specialise in the functions of command and especially in co-ordination. It is difficult to see how in any large enterprise the increased specialisation which is necessary for effective administration under modern conditions can be reconciled with a clear-cut distribution of authority and responsibility, without some such device to secure co-ordination without overburdening the chief. It may therefore be stated as a principle of organisation that

*Executive Control involves as its primary responsibility the co-ordination of the work of subordinates exercising unitary and functional responsibilities. In any large undertaking this postulates a " staff " system.*

## V

" The assertion that these great industrial organisations owe their success to administrative genius appears to be true in many cases. The real point, however, is that it would have to be true in every case if there were no such thing as principles of organisation. Without these principles, all operations of any magnitude would be absolutely dependent for their creation and permanence on administrative genius of corresponding magnitude, and could not hope long to survive the removal of such genius. It seems needless to observe that this has not been the usual history of human organisations of any kind. . . . If the principles of organisation we have asserted are real and not imaginary, then their correct application must contain the solvent of all such problems. Given this application it is impossible to conceive of any human organisation too vast for organised efficiency. Such organisations, even the greatest, can get along without that exceptional thing we call genius if they are grounded on sound, proved and tested principles."—J. D. MOONEY and A. C. REILEY, *Onward Industry*.

# CHAPTER V

## THE ORGANISATION OF COMPLEX BUSINESS ENTERPRISES

IN the general field of organisation the complex business enterprise, with large branches
operating at considerable distances from head-
quarters or formed by some degree of fusion of
previously independent undertakings, constitutes a
special case.

Since the year 1920 there has been a very
rapid growth in the number of business undertakings which have resulted from some degree of combination between previously independent enterprises. Many such undertakings operate internationally. It is likely that this tendency will
continue. The development among business-men
of all countries of the general complex of ideas
represented by the word " Rationalisation " has
engendered an inclination to view favourably the
possibility of collaboration with others trading in
the same commodities, and a readiness to suppress
the personal objections which hinder such collaboration. The obvious wastes of " cut-throat "
competition, both on the national and on the international plane, thrust themselves more and more
into the foreground. It becomes increasingly

obvious that while some degree of rivalry between individual enterprises is healthy and beneficial and while the variety and complexity of consumer demand cannot be regimented, at the same time there are large areas of business activity in which the co-ordinated pursuit of a common policy operates to the benefit of all concerned. It means more profit to the producer, more stable employment at higher wages for the worker, and a lower price to the consumer.

The same lesson is enforced by the technical progress of modern productive methods. While no serious attempt has been made as yet to present statistically the costs of complexity, there is a widespread recognition that the factory which attempts to produce a wide variety of products at the behest of the more old-fashioned type of salesman is hopelessly handicapped. It is sometimes urged that, as far as Europe is concerned, the richness and variety of her national cultures, coupled with the hindrance to commerce imposed by national tariffs, definitely inhibit her from achieving the full advantages of mass production. This is only partially true. There are certain rather outstanding and dramatic cases in which the minimum output for maximum efficiency in manufacture is extremely high. Automobiles are a case in point. But for the larger proportion of consumer goods and, too, for a large variety of manufacturers' goods, the unit of maximum efficiency for manufacturing purposes is not so large as to transcend the market possibilities of the majority of the

European countries. That is to say, provided the factory can specialise in single articles and patterns on standard lines, a comparatively small plant can achieve quite as striking economies as larger competitors.

It is rather from the direction of finance and distribution that the pressure towards amalgamation comes in such cases. Where the article manufactured is a unit of small value it is not worth while to develop a modern sales organisation with all the contingent expense for a comparatively small turnover. Representatives cannot call on all the retailers concerned unless the range of goods that they are selling is wide enough to secure a minimum order in money values sufficient to pay the cost of the visit. Where the article manufactured is of a specialised character involving installation work or after-sales service for maintenance, it is again impossible to maintain the necessary distributive organisation except on the basis of a large turnover.

For all these reasons the movement towards collaboration continues. The forms in which it issues vary very greatly. The structure, particularly of international combinations, is deeply affected by the historical processes underlying their foundation.

While this general movement is likely to prove both profitable to those concerned and beneficial to the community, it is open to certain dangers. Public attention tends to concentrate on the risk that such large amalgamations may issue in monopolistic tendencies and the extraction of unreasonable profits. But this current in public opinion is certainly less marked than in the past, and has probably always been exaggerated. The main danger which may be anticipated from these large-scale combinations is a different one. A number of economists have called attention to the risk that they may prove incapable in future of procuring the necessary talent for the conduct of their administration. This opinion is expressed not so much by economists of a radical temperament, but by those who are most clearly attracted by the flexibility and initiative resulting from the smaller scale individualist enterprise of the last century.[1]

These apprehensions are, of course, not wholly unreasonable, and have some foundation in the failure of business men up to the present time to interest themselves in the principles of combine administration. It is now nearly half a century since F. W. Taylor first laid the foundations for the scientific study of the control of the single undertaking or shop. His work has been constantly developed since that date by engineers and research students in all parts of the world. The Management Engineer faced with the organisation chart of an individual enterprise can discuss the facts revealed intelligently in the light of principle, irrespective of any personal knowledge, either of the technical processes involved in the particular industry or of the personalities of the individuals hold-

[1] J. H. Jones, *Economics of Private Enterprise*, p. 124. London : Pitman & Sons, Ltd.

ing the various positions. That is not to say that knowledge of these latter factors is not of great advantage. But he is in the same position as a Mechanical Engineer considering the drawing of a machine without reference to the nature of the substances on which the machine is to operate or of the material of which its parts are to be composed, but who can nevertheless point out the features in its structure which are questionable from the standpoint of engineering principle.

When faced, however, with the large-scale amalgamation, and particularly with amalgamations of all types in the international field, the Management Engineer has no such background of principle on which to work. Nor is there at present any evidence that the importance of this problem has been fully appreciated by the large amalgamations themselves. Very little literature has appeared upon it. Indeed, with the exception of a study of the organisation of General Motors Limited recently issued by the American Management Association,[1] work of a practical character is almost negligible.

There has, of course, been a large amount of literature issued on the growth of various forms of amalgamation, and particularly on international cartels, but this work has been directed almost entirely to the economic aspects of these forms of combination. The published material deals

[1] Edgar W. Smith, *Organisation and Operating Principles* (issued by the American Management Association, New York).

with the character of the different industries combined, the nature of the arrangements made for bringing them together, the terms on which quotas are based for cartel purposes, the accountancy technique in arriving at valuation for the purpose of combination, and so on. It does not attempt to touch the special problems in administration and management which arise when combination has taken place.

It may be urged that sound principles of administration are the same whether for a single company or for many, or for a combination of many previously independent companies, or indeed that they are the same for large-scale undertakings of all kinds whether these are engaged in business or other activities. This is, to some degree, true, but only partially so. And even a superficial study of such business combinations reveals immediately a series of administrative difficulties which are special to such combinations and require intensive and special study.

The most important of such issues are concerned with questions such as the composition of the controlling Board or other authority, the amount of centralisation of control which shall take place, the functions of the business to which such centralised control shall be applied, the degree of local initiative allowed to subordinate managers, the arrangements for securing that the degree of control which has been determined upon shall in fact be realised, and so on.

In a recent enquiry conducted by the International Management Institute into twenty large combinations, it appeared that there was an almost rhythmical movement of policy with regard to the question of centralisation and decentralisation. In some instances the combinations when brought about had started off to centralise violently all the functions hitherto exercised by the independent units. But it was discovered rapidly that this process is destructive of local and individual initiative and of that flexibility which is the cardinal virtue of business undertakings. There followed a period of complete decentralisation, but this again revealed the fact that most of the anticipated advantages of common action and common policy were thereby lost. The majority of the undertakings examined had arrived at no clear view of principles bearing on this vital question.

The same consideration holds true, *mutatis mutandis*, of looser forms of amalgamation such as cartels, standardisation work on products or costs, and so on. Certain cartels have succeeded ; others have failed. It is usually urged that the failures were due to economic causes. But they may equally have been due to administrative causes. That is to say, the machinery set up for the actual administration of such elements of common action as were determined upon in the cartel arrangement may have been at fault, the friction which developed among the members being due to this cause rather than to any degree of economic pressure sufficient to account for the breakdown of the cartel. Some trades have been extremely successful in establishing standard costing systems or in setting up machinery for the simplification of products or the standardisation of measurements and processes : others have been glaringly unsuccessful in similar attempts. Here again, economic reasons are usually adduced to account for the difficulties encountered. But it is equally possible that maladministration may again have been the real cause of the disturbance.

For all these reasons it is suggested that if the movement towards Rationalisation is to win for the world community the advantages which are claimed for it, the process must be carried farther and deeper than has hitherto been appreciated. Merely to combine previously independent undertakings, either wholly or partially, is not to rationalise their administration. It is merely to create an opportunity for so doing. Whether that opportunity will in the long run and over the whole area of business activity be adequately realised, depends to a very large degree on the extent to which the technique of Scientific Management which has proved so beneficial in the case of the individual business can also be applied to the larger problems of administration raised by the combination.

If scientifically determined principles of permanent validity are to be substituted for the present empirical method of dealing with these issues, a large task of research awaits the business world. There is already available a large body of experience in the conduct and administration of combinations, both nationally and internationally. Many such undertakings have been conducted with outstanding success over a long period of years. But the history of their administrative methods is lost in their minute books, their accounts, and the veil of secrecy drawn by discretion across some of their earlier mistakes. In the words of one of Mr. Kipling's characters, they have " muddied the wells of enquiry with the stick of precaution ". At the same time, it is improbable that large-scale businesses can evade the necessity of a scientific study of the principles of combined administration, particularly in the international field.

Such study, if it is to be scientific, must be inductive. At the moment material for such an inductive study does not exist. But it can be created, given international collaboration, and the necessary resources. All that is necessary is that some two or three hundred of the largest combines should be studied from the standpoint of their methods of administration and management on a standard scheme. The purpose of such study should not be critical but designed to obtain a brief statement of the essential facts. Nor need it reveal any material of importance to competitors. Administration is not concerned with the technical secrets which are properly reserved by many under-takings, but with the method of dealing with problems which are common to all large concerns. There would be no direct need to publish the material, provided it could be made available for serious students under suitable safeguards. Though, as a matter of fact, in cases where undertakings interested themselves in such an investigation and were given opportunities of preventing the issue of any statements to which they objected, they would probably be glad to issue a report, which might indeed have a high publicity value.

The main difficulty at the moment is a material one. Few undertakings have realised the value to themselves of such a study of their administration and the far greater values to be achieved by collaborating with others and by the general pooling of experience. While they will often in individual cases spend very large sums of money on trying to obtain the necessary information to solve a particular problem which is troubling them at the moment, the more fundamental research necessary to put most of such problems in the way of solution for the future at a far smaller cost does not appeal to them.

On the other hand, the amount of international contact for research purposes is constantly on the increase. Students and post-graduate workers are constantly passing between Europe and the United States and between the different European countries. Many of them are engaged on economic or sociological investigations on subjects which they have selected for no very well defined reason. Often these subjects are far too wide and too generalised for effective results to be obtained. They would contribute far more seriously to the general solution of economic problems if their work could be organised and directed so as to contribute by research into a given undertaking on standard lines to the general establishment of scientific principles for the control of combinations. The organisations which financed them would bê spending their money to better advantage, and the investigators themselves would find that their researches had given them a larger grip, both on general conditions in other countries and on business administration as a subject.

In any event the problem of the administration of the large-scale business combination is one which, in the interests of business men themselves, calls for the widest measure of international collaboration and of intensive research.

# PART THREE

## DISTRIBUTION

## VI

" The purpose of business is to get wealth to people—to produce and to distribute to all humanity the things which humanity, with its new-found power, can now be organised to make only if it can be organised to buy and use them."— E. A. FILENE, *Successful Living in this Machine Age.*

" The correct focus on modern industry is unattainable until we recognise that distribution is its great unsolved problem."—J. D. MOONEY and A. C. REILEY, *Onward Industry.*

# CHAPTER VI

## THE MARKETING POINT OF VIEW

THE question which now faces the industrialised nations is not primarily a question of how to produce their requirements. It is how to organise the distribution of what they have produced and can produce. If the present acute financial crisis is regarded in simple terms —and like all great issues it is simple, and only to be understood if treated simply—it is in effect a colossal failure on an international scale to understand and to arrange for the processes of distribution.

The crisis is called a financial crisis. But what is finance? Men are accustomed to talk about business activities as if they were divisible into three main groups : production, distribution, and finance. But this is a deceptive analysis. It is true that there are three groups, three aspects of business activity which are of first importance. But the third aspect, finance, is totally different in character to the other two. Production and distribution are realities : they are concerned with the fundamental purpose of all economic life, to supply and to deliver the goods and services which men and women require. But finance is not concerned directly with these realities ; viewed broadly, it is a secondary, a facilitative activity, concerned with assisting in the other two fundamental processes. No amount of money has ever of itself produced a loaf of bread or conveyed it to a human being who wished to eat it.

The present financial mechanisms by which the world's business is conducted are extremely complex. Every variety of habit pattern has been built up around them. Half the world's ideas about business are based on them. They are the centre of a whole complex of traditions, organised activity and vested authorities, and these things are hard to change. But unless and until men become simpler, unless they are prepared to realise that they have elevated a servant into a master, have made of a facilitative service a major function, they have no prospect of getting out of their difficulties. The function of industry and commerce is to produce and to distribute. That is their major purpose. Until that major purpose is viewed directly, and not through a prism of finance, those who control industry and commerce will not be the men who make and supply goods, but the men who run the financial services, the scorers. And since quite a number of advantages can be secured by exacting a premium on those services—it would perhaps be unduly harsh to say by faking the score—it is hardly surprising if control from this angle sometimes gets production and distribution into a mess.

A further consideration is that this control of business by its servant could not have taken place had the two partners in the business game understood each other and their respective jobs. And since it is manifestly not the power to produce which is at fault, it follows that the muddle must have occurred either in the processes of distribution or in the correlation of distribution with production.

How has this come about? The explanation is a fairly simple one. A hundred years ago, before power production with all its consequences had come to complicate economic arrangements, the producer and distributor were the same person. The work of distribution was carried out, as it is today, for certain types of agricultural and other produce, by means of markets ; a market or fair was simply a fixed place and time where buyers and sellers could meet.

The processes which were carried out by means of the markets of a more primitive period were the same as those cared for by the complex mechanisms of today. In the first place, the producer knew that on the market day at the local market town he would find all the potential customers, all the " prospects " for his particular product. By bringing his products to the market he performed the first half of the total cycle of activities called transportation. In doing this he behaved exactly as a manufacturer of today behaves when he delivers his goods to a retail establishment or agent. That function of the primitive market is adequately cared for by the present economic organisation.

In the second place, arrived at the market, he displayed his goods on a stall or stand where people who might want to buy them could see them readily. If he was a pushful fellow he also made a noise to call attention to himself and his goods. That is to say, he advertised them. Today, with postal facilities, printing, the popular Press, radio (except in Great Britain), window display experts and shopping weeks, there are all sorts of new facilities for taking care of this elemental function of Distribution.

When the early producer had carried his goods to market and had displayed them, there followed the process of sale centring round the question of price. Customers passed by his stall. If they stopped and started to bargain, he became aware immediately of the possibilities of sale within a definite price range. With the exception, however, of this greater flexibility with regard to price adjustments, his action in this respect differed little from that of the travelling salesman of today whose bag of samples or book of quotations is the basis of sale across the retailer's counter or purchasing agent's desk.

But there was one function, one need, which the producer-consumer-tradesman satisfied by attendance at the primitive market which the present practice of distribution at a distance has largely failed to replace. From the talk of customers about his stall, from a glance at the stalls of other vendors, from the gossip which characterised the " ordinary " at the local inn, he learned a vital series of facts. He absorbed almost unconsciously a grasp of all that material which is now called market information. He knew almost precisely the quality and quantity of competitive effort which he would have to meet. Defects in his own products, whether as to design, quality or price, were brought home to him immediately either by indifference or by homely comment. The nature, volume and direction of demand were developing under his nose. Since his production was essentially hand production for immediate needs he returned home to his workshop for another spell as a producer with a very lively and intimate sense of what was required of him. He *knew*, not what a design department thought would be acceptable, but what king customer *was* accepting ; not what price his cost accountant told him he should get, but the price which, next week or next month, he *could* get ; not how much he would like to make to keep his factory running at capacity, but how much he *would have* to make to satisfy the existing demand. That is to say, his actions as a producer were dominated in their every aspect by this directly absorbed knowledge of the needs of the consumer.

This picture is, of course, over-simplified. But it represents fairly definitely the position at the dawn of the industrial revolution. That sudden and tremendous accretion in productive capacity encountered a world still largely under-supplied, as are great areas of the world today, with the most elementary necessities of civilisation. As a consequence, there was almost a century of a pronounced sellers' market. There were ups and downs, of course. But by and large the main problems facing business were concerned with the development of the new means of production and of transportation. This development has produced the world as it is today, a world in which on the whole business men have taken to thinking of production first and of distribution afterwards. They have come to regard the main function of distribution as selling what production happens to make. In this connection they have enormously developed the first three functions of the original market, transporting, selling and advertising.

In doing so, they have to a large degree lost sight of the main function of those earlier markets—the informational function. The main job of distribution is not to get rid of what production makes, it is to tell production what it ought to make. It is as the nervous system of economic life that distribution should play its vital and controlling part in the economic order. Fundamentally business is suffering from a serious functional disorder of the nervous system.

It may be argued that that is an exaggerated picture. Salesmen are in touch with retailers or agents ; advertising people undertake market research ; there are all kinds of statistics bearing on sales ; business realises that it has to satisfy its customers and that it would be crazy to manufacture except to satisfy a market. All this is true. But it does not bring prosperity. Retailers and agents are not consumers ; they are intermediate distributors. Their knowledge of consumer demand and its laws is frequently twisted by the desire to have something with their name on it, or something that the fellow across the road has not got. Market Research, while of supreme value to the individual manufacturer, is almost always undertaken with a view, not to finding out what the consumer's habits really are, but to selling what some particular manufacturer can make. Statistics of sales, while extremely valuable in analysing the past and directing current distributive effort in detail, reveal nothing whatever about the future. Business pays lip-service to the importance of the consumer. But usually it only knows who its customers have been and what they have done. It has no notion who its potential consumers will be and what they will do.

Not only have the growth of machine production and modern communications destroyed the sensitive and direct relationship between manufacturer and consumer, they have also made the necessity for a more sensitive relationship much greater. This has occurred in three different ways.

In the first place, the technique of machine manufacture has altered the conditions of production. Rarely is manufacturing conducted to meet definite needs expressed in orders. Business manufactures in advance for stock. Moreover, the more can be manufactured of a single article, the more production can be simplified, the lower are costs. There is, as yet, an imperfect conception of the possibilities in this direction. The majority still look at manufacturing costs first and the market second. Ford's whole success in the motor industry is fundamentally due to a reversal of that process. He asked himself first the question : at what price must I put a car on the market to sell half a million or a million ? Then he turned his whole energy to making a car at that price. The success of such firms as Woolworth's or Marks & Spencer is again due to a definite realisation of this simple principle. They have created mass-distribution machinery which enables them to secure the sale of all sorts of articles by the hundred thousand or the million, *provided that the price is right.* They then go to the manufacturer and say : we will give you a firm order for a very large quantity at such and such a price. And when the manufacturer looks at unit costs in the old-fashioned way, and says he cannot do it, they are quite prepared to send a cost accountant into his works to show him how it can be done.

Distribution costs, in the sense of the actual expense which occurs between the factory and the consumer, are undoubtedly too high in many instances. But this is due to the low efficiency of the marginal distributor rather than to any deliberate profiteering on the part of more efficient distributors. The problem of price-cutting in many trades is definitely due to the existence of this wide gap between the most efficient and least efficient distributor. Big reforms are needed in this field. Scientific management must be applied to the whole range of distributive processes, as it has been to productive work. But there is a risk that too great concentration on detailed costs may conceal the more important issue. Methods of distribution, even where they cost more, which are mass methods and therefore enable machine production to operate to its full efficiency, are the greatest source of economy open to the world today.

In the second place, the higher standard of living which is characteristic of a number of countries since the introduction of machine methods has definitely made the market more uncertain. Where two individuals, A and B, are earning what may be called a subsistence wage, roughly ninety per cent. of their expenditure will be devoted to necessities—shelter, clothing and food. And within any given national group the forms which such expenditure will take are fairly easy to predict and are difficult to change by advertising or other means. It is well known that consumption of bread in the British market is relatively inelastic —that is to say, it varies little in response to a general rise or fall in the retail price of the loaf. It is a staple necessity. Where, however, A and B have a subsistence wage plus fifty per cent. or one hundred per cent., the amount of that wage devoted to subsistence remains roughly constant. But the additional fifty or one hundred per cent. is added to the total volume of optional expenditure, expenditure whose direction is determined by the personal choice of the consumer and may be highly erratic. This condition of the larger proportion of total expenditure which is optional is responsible for what is called " the new competition "—that is, the replacement of direct competition between manufacturers making the same article by competition between manufacturers making quite different articles for a larger share of the consumer's pound. It is perhaps the underlying cause of the severity of the present depression in the United States of America.

In the third place, modern methods of communication have made industry and trade in fact, if not in appearance, international.

But the effect of this growing internationalisation has been to expose the markets for commodities and services to all kinds of influences from which the local market for basic necessities was relatively immune. These influences are both economic, that is to say, they are concerned with the actual organisation of business, and extraneous. The extraneous influences are such emotions as national feeling expressing itself in economic imperialism, political considerations leading to legislation designed to please specific interests or classes, or fear leading to uneconomic arrangements designed to facilitate the situation of particular groups in the event of war. The economic influences include group selfishness leading to uneconomic efforts to bolster up particular productive equipment, and particularly the inter-dependence of the world financial system leading to great sensitiveness with regard to credit and the confidence on which it is based. A break in that confidence is, of course, one of the roots of the present troubles.

While the two sets of causes are almost inextricable in any given instance they are clearly distinguishable. Could the world forget for a moment its national feelings, its political or sectional or class prejudices and its fears, could its statesmen sit down quietly to solve the problem of supplying the world as a business problem, it would not prove so complicated or so unamenable to scientific knowledge and method. Incidentally everyone would be more prosperous.

The situation is no one's fault. There are no scapegoats. The tendency observable recently in certain countries to look for scapegoats—America sometimes calls them " alibis "—is the most serious psychological feature of the present situation. The world has adopted in the last hundred years a totally new technique for meeting its material requirements. People have shown themselves collectively slow in adapting their economic methods to that technique. That technique has first broken the natural contact between producer and consumer found in the early market. At the same time, it has made the penalties of misjudgment of demand more severe. It has made demand itself more erratic, and by extending the area in which it operates, it has made it more vulnerable to outside influences.

If this analysis is correct, if the long sellers' market, coupled with the development of machine production, have resulted in the growth of an incorrect point of view so that business always thinks about production first and distribution second, the first and most essential thing is to break that habit.

Bad habits, incorrect ways of looking at problems, usually express themselves in organisation, and one of the ways of curing them is by changes in organisation. Moreover, if it is true that as a result of that bad habit producers have neglected to supply mechanisms in modern factories to replace the touch with the market of the earlier hand producer, there is an obvious practical need which requires attention.

The majority of business enterprises are organised in three main divisions—production, selling, and finance. Generally speaking, co-ordination between these divisions is arranged for by conference under the chairmanship of the General Manager or Managing Director. Now, such an arrangement is perfectly adequate if the job of distribution is regarded as selling what production makes. But if the first task of distribution is to indicate to production what it should make, at what price and in what quantity, it leaves the daily responsibility for a large number of decisions of vital importance to the business inadequately defined and sometimes unprovided for altogether.

The first thing to be done is, therefore, the creation in every business of a new and separate main division of responsibilities and duties which may be called the " marketing division ". The tasks which should be allocated to such a division are numerous and varied ; they may be described broadly as all those questions which arise in securing adequate co-ordination between manufacturing and selling. They include :

(*a*) Determining what the business shall make and sell, how many different lines and how many different sizes or patterns.

(*b*) Determining the price at which the business shall sell them. Is it more profitable to sell *x* units at ten shillings each, or *x* plus fifty units at eight shillings each ? This, of course, includes countless detailed decisions as to price policy.

(*c*) Determining to whom the business can and should sell them. This, of course, involves market research and the development of new avenues and methods of distribution.

(*d*) Determining when lines should be added or withdrawn. This includes the study of the demand so as to suggest directions in which the range may be improved, or to give an informed judgment on suggestions from other quarters. It also includes direct responsibility for seeing that the supply of new products is adequate both as regards frequency and design to secure the established market and the winning of new markets. It also includes all the detailed arrangements necessary to ensure that when a new line is launched the efforts of all departments of the business, design, production, advertising and selling, are united behind the new venture, focussed as to time, quantity, and range of effort.

(*e*) If this duty is to be fulfilled satisfactorily, it involves a constant and systematic study of the products and methods of competitors.

(*f*) Determining the quantities at which the business should aim in the sale of each of its lines. This involves economic study of general business trends, of the specific conditions and trends in the given industry and enterprise, of local variations in general trends, and so on. From such studies should issue the general budget on which sales and production plans are based.

(*g*) Determination of the standard of quality which the business should seek to maintain.

This marketing division or department should not be placed " over " production and sales. It should be a parallel department with its own clearly defined duties and functions of a planning and co-ordinating type, such as have been indicated. In the event of failure in adjustment, the Managing Director should continue to exercise his function of control as at present. Nor is a very large staff required. Some research workers, a small clerical staff, three or four sub-managers, should meet the requirements of even a large business. But the chief of the department should be the best subordinate manager with the most initiative, imagination, foresight and commercial judgment whom the managing director has available.

It may be urged that all these duties and functions are already being attended to by someone. No business can continue if they are not. But the point is that duties which are attended to by someone as an appendix to other preoccupations are usually carried out anyhow. The question of the composition of the price-list is an example. The man who is primarily interested in production naturally presses for simplicity, if he knows anything about the economies of machine processing. The man who is primarily responsible for selling naturally and inevitably presses for constant novelty and a wide range of choice. It is easier to sell. All too frequently there is a conflict of these two specialised interests. A busy managing director is called in to make a snap decision if he is a strong man, or to suggest a compromise if he is of a more accommodating character, when what is wanted is continuous and detailed study designed to integrate all the various considerations involved into a progressive and unified policy.

Such unification is a continuous job. It is not a matter of occasional decision. And it can only be carried out effectively and satisfactorily if there are definite organs, live organs, within the organism specialised for that purpose. Imagine a man whose nervous system only functioned intermittently, or whose limbs went about their business without reference to his senses !

This suggestion involves nothing more than providing specialised parts of any business organisation to carry out those functions of the early market, which in the pressure of the industrial revolution have been forgotten. As the sub-division of labour has proceeded, the manufacturing and the transport and the selling activities of the original handicraft producer-distributor have been replaced by complex and highly articulated special departments. The knowledge which he absorbed when he went to market has been overlooked. And if the principle of specialisation on which business has proceeded is right, it cannot fill the gap by tacking this function rather vaguely on to the duties of other specialists. It must provide for it specifically and effectively.

If this course is taken, it meets the main difficulties which have been described. The existence of a strong and effective marketing department in any business will not only provide in practice for more constant study and clearer decisions on those imponderables on which the most vital factors in prosperity are largely based. In addition, it will focus the thought of all concerned afresh. They will be brought to appreciate that before production is undertaken or selling can begin, there is a prior process—the study of the market and the determination of what is to be done. They will redress the balance of their thought and approach distribution questions from the correct angle—an angle which no longer takes the factory for granted, and sees what can be done about it—but goes back of the factory to the consumer, appreciating that no productive effort is justified save as a direct response to existing or potential demand.

It will also do much, as much as can be done, to secure the machine producer against the greatly increased risks of manufacturing in advance. In many markets, especially those concerned with

H

consumer goods, it is difficult, if not impossible, to forecast sales in advance with complete accuracy. In the case of producers' goods it is on the whole easier. Where it is difficult no one is very willing to undertake the job of guessing. It becomes divided up among a number of departments who make *ad hoc* adjustments following the actual trend of sales. This is convenient in the sense that no individual bears the responsibility for the very expensive consequences of guessing wrong. But in effect the guess has been made all the same. After all, the factory has to produce something. It is much better that a specified individual should be charged with this responsibility of making a forward estimate, and that the higher control should view with a wide elasticity the inevitable cases when that estimate is falsified by events.

Such a marketing department will go as far as lies within the power of the individual concern towards solving the problem created by the increased instability of large areas of demand, due to the fact that they are concerned with that greater proportion of the consumer's income which is available for optional expenditure. The last main difficulty was the greater vulnerability of demand due to the international character of business and its consequent susceptibility to general waves of economic optimism or pessimism and to political influences.

In both these cases the individual manufacturer is dealing with factors partly or largely outside his control. As an individual he can do no more than strive his utmost to keep in touch with the facts and take all possible steps within his own competence to neutralise adverse influences. In connection with general economic movements he can, at least, have the available figures before him. And if he studies them objectively, he will be doing something to secure that his decisions, as far as his business is concerned, are not influenced by that general mass suggestion which does so much to exaggerate the effects of the trade cycle.

In addition the manufacturer can do a great deal in his corporate capacities as a member of his trade and as a citizen of his country. Co-operative advertising and co-operative exploitation of export markets, co-operative research into market factors, and the elimination of overlapping as between the research departments of advertising agencies and other organisations which are trying to throw light on distribution—in all these directions there are opportunities for combined action. They will be considered in a later chapter.

Judging by their published statistics, there is not a single Government in Europe which has yet grasped the elementary fact that business depends on consumption. Measurement of income, of purchasing power, of its distribution by areas, classes and commodities, of the channels of distribution and their relative importance—all these vital facts are lacking. Till the manufacturer has them, he must go on guessing—and inevitably guessing wrong. As trader and as citizen he has a double line of attack on these larger problems.

As citizen he can at least do his utmost to curb the national emotions and political prejudices which cut across economic development.  He can demand that every policy be put to the acid test —does it or does it not tend towards a higher standard of living for the people ?  On the achievement of that higher standard his life as a business man depends.

## VII

" It is now fairly well understood that the processes of mass distribution—that necessary concomitant of mass production—are far from being as highly developed or as perfect in technique as production itself. Certain aspects of the distributive mechanism in Great Britain represent a stage which would correspond on the manufacturing side to the cottage industries of the eighteenth century. Yet side by side with this anachronism there are growing up distributive instrumentalities and processes which belong properly to the modern world. The clash between the two constitutes a very serious problem for the manufacturer in his rôle as a seller of goods."—G. HARRISON, Introduction to *Market Research* by Paul Redmayne and Hugh Weeks.

# CHAPTER VII

## MANUFACTURER AND DISTRIBUTOR

IT was suggested in the last chapter that during the past hundred years the world has adopted a technique for meeting its material requirements which is completely new. That technique has first broken the natural contact between producer and consumer found in the early market. At the same time it has made the penalties of misjudgment of demand more severe. It has made demand itself more erratic and by extending the area in which it operates, it has made it more vulnerable to outside influences.

If that is a correct analysis it follows that the critical point in the whole mechanism of distribution is the point of contact between buyer and seller. It is not only critical, but extremely sensitive. *Caveat emptor* has been the motto of competitive business from time immemorial. Today the world is in the middle of a revolution in its distributive methods. New forms of distributive organisation, department stores, chain stores, chains of department stores, co-operatives, manufacturers' retailing, one price shops, national advertising of branded goods, daily deliveries from local depots, are evolving in every country as rapidly as the new power-driven factories replaced the handicraft workshops and domestic manufacture at the beginning of the industrial revolution. The old handicraft distributors, wholesalers, agents, commission men, small retailers and so on are suffering in security and livelihood exactly as the handicraft workers suffered when the machines came. The new large-scale buyer for retail sale is in a position of suddenly acquired economic power. So, in the market for industrial goods, is the modern large combination of manufacturing businesses. And inevitably relations on each side of the critical point are strained. Individuals are apprehensive, resentful, and difficult to deal with.

Specialisation of the selling processes through wholesalers and retailers has not only removed the manufacturer from direct contact with consumers. It has placed him in a seller-buyer relationship with those who are in such contact. On both sides there is an inevitable tendency to concentrate attention on this relationship since adjustments either way at this point, particularly with regard to price, are reflected directly in profit. The process of forecasting the future of demand is divided between two or more independent traders each of whom is primarily concerned with avoiding mistakes in his particular calculations rather than with the accuracy of the forecast as a whole.

The immediate interests of the two groups from the technical standpoint have also tended to drift apart. More and more producers have come to appreciate the economy of a simplified range of products which will facilitate long machine runs on a small range of articles or processes. Distributors, on the other hand, are preoccupied with satisfying the requirements of consumers which are often fickle and uncertain. Their task is necessarily to present the widest possible range of choice in type, pattern, size and variety of goods to potential purchasers.

The independence of the two groups has also introduced an intangible element of conflict centring round goodwill. The producer wishes to impress his " brand " as a supplier on the minds of consumers. The distributor wishes to emphasise his name as standing for an efficient service.

Power-driven machine methods have evolved very rapidly, leading to an enormous increase in the volume and variety of goods produced. At the same time the general causes enumerated have made such production less and less sensitive to the detailed aspects of effective demand. The loss in productive equipment caused by four and a half years of war was made good within a decade. The world's productive capacity in 1929 was higher than in 1913. But the dislocation caused to trading arrangements, that is to the distributive mechanism, which depends very largely on knowledge, confidence, well-established relationships between producer and distributor and similar intangibles, has not been made good. The business system has broken down at what was already in process of becoming its weakest link, the adjustment of supply to demand.

It was assumed that the economic argument that there could not be such a thing as over-production, that if more was produced more would be available for exchange and everyone would be better off, was universal. The economic argument is still correct in general. Obviously the world's needs are far from being fulfilled. It is inapplicable in detail. More production is futile if it is production of the wrong things at the wrong times and places in the wrong quantities at the wrong prices and under arrangements which do not permit the producers, viewed as consumers, to buy what they have produced. This failure of adjustment is of particular importance to individual business undertakings because it is the part of the total problem which they can attack directly by their own action.

How can the manufacturer help the distributor?

In the first place the manufacturer can use every avenue of research open to him to secure that the goods which he offers are really those which the consumer needs. He can avoid forcing the distributor by mass advertising and by selling pressure, to stock lines which do not represent the consumer's view of what he wants, but the manufacturer's view of what he ought to want.

One of the consequences of the domination of the production standpoint in the recent past has undoubtedly been an exaggerated respect paid to the manufacturing expert. The point of view of the man who spends his life making a given article as to its quality and desirability differs inevitably from that of the consumer who seeks a casual and often temporary satisfaction from it. A greater readiness to measure consumer opinion practically and statistically will do something to safeguard the producer against the highly erratic tendencies of modern demand and will assist his relations with distributors.

Where an active marketing department, such as was described in the last chapter, has been established, special attention is necessary from this standpoint. In the case of one very scientifically managed factory the marketing staff were extremely fertile in devising new uses for its products and means of persuading the public to accept them. As long as times were good all went well. But the new uses were all catchy, amusing ideas that appealed to the optional surplus of the consumer's pound and a larger and larger percentage of the company's increasing sales were in this field. When depression came and the public had no optional surpluses, too high a proportion of sales were affected immediately.

In the second place the manufacturer can secure that the goods which he produces are not so varied as to force the retailer to carry an uneconomic range of stock or advertised in a way which confuses rather than enlightens the consumer.

An example of the results of these tendencies is the story of an English couple who were visiting Geneva. The wife had promised the husband a wrist-watch for a present. Geneva is of course the Mecca of the watchmakers. When they had visited fifteen shops and been shown fifty or sixty different wrist-watches in each, at as many price-levels, they took stock. They were forced to the conclusion that they knew nothing whatever about buying time-keeping machinery, and that the manufacturers had taken no steps to teach them. They were averse to buying a watch on its coachwork. So the husband said, " My dear, Mr. Dunhill has made pipe-buying safe for women. I'll let you off with a guinea ". The practice of the automobile industry in educating the public through its advertising to buy from specification is a more scientific procedure.

The point which causes the maximum misunderstanding and failure in collaboration at the moment is price-cutting. A manufacturer creates a market for a branded article at a fixed selling price. Some retailer finds that he can get along with a big turnover at a small profit margin, and secures the turnover by cutting the fixed selling price. Immediately all the other retailers are irritated. The more ardently they support in theory the principles of competition and individualism, the more anxious they appear in practice to curtail the price-cutter's liberty and to substitute the rules of the prize-ring for those more customary in commercial rivalry. Every kind of effort is made to use force in some form or other to compel him to conform.

Now of course there is price-cutting and price-cutting. There is the individual who builds up a big trade on cut-prices in a chain of shops in order to sell them to the widow and to the orphan who do not know enough about accounting to distinguish between turnover and net profit. There is the retailer who puts in one well-known branded line as a " loss leader " to bring customers into his shop. The first is a swindler. The second is perhaps employing an undesirable form of trading. He is creating a false impression on the public in order to get rid of goods ; his action is comparable with unethical advertising. But genuine, successful and consistent price-cutting is simply a warning to the rest of the trade that gross profit margins on retailing are too high, or alternatively that the spread between quantity and normal terms offered by the manufacturer is too wide for his goods to be suitable for the small retailer.

In any event, in a country which is free politically and economically, force is no great use in dealing with the problem. It can only be tackled effectively by research, particularly research into the structure of the distributive costs of the trade. Such research again must be mutual, conducted either by the trade association or by universities or other research institutions working in conjunction with the trade association. Only by detailed, painstaking, accurate and comparative analysis of the costs of a large number of traders is it possible to determine whether a case of price-cutting is sound competitive trading which should be regarded as a warning to the rest, or an aberration. Where it is an aberration it may safely be left to the cure of loss ; where it is a warning it is for the trade as a whole to consider whether its standard of distributive efficiency does not require to be worked up.

In any event the cure is research ; organised knowledge rather than organised violence is the only basis on which the bad elements in price-cutting can be kept within bounds. Moreover, such co-operative research into the elements of distributive cost would largely prevent price-cutting altogether. No one trades at a loss for fun : many, driven by competition or the results of their own bad management, trade at a loss through ignorance. The printing-trade of Great Britain was driven towards universal bankruptcy before the war by internecine price-cutting. Some of its more far-sighted employers induced their fellows to introduce and to use a standard costing system. The trouble disappeared almost completely. This is an example of the way knowledge works to eliminate difficulties which are too often attributed to depravity, instead of to their correct source, ignorance.

The manufacturer can help the distributor also in a direct attack on the wastes due to an excessive variety of products. The work achieved by the Bureau of Simplification at Washington is a case in point. There is no possible advantage to the world in having 170 different kinds of chopper to choose from at 10s. instead of 10 kinds at 2s. The amount of sheer unnecessary waste caused by thoughtless competitive selling is appalling. The number of varieties of all kinds of goods can be reduced without loss to anyone. There will be great gains to the manufacturer in production economies, to all types of distributors in eliminating unnecessary investment and slow-moving stocks, and to the consumer in price. But the work of simplifying can only be carried through as the result of the most meticulous market research conducted by representatives of all three parties acting in co-operation. The advantages can only be retained by loyal adherence to agreements by all concerned.

Above all the manufacturer can help the distributor by basing the work of such a marketing department as was described in the previous chapter on real knowledge of the facts. Confusion and uncertainty of policy within a manufacturing undertaking are reflected in unreliability and caprice in its relations with distributors. The same division of interests from the technical standpoint occurs between producing and selling departments, as between manufacturers and retailers. The one wants long machine runs, the other variety and novelty of product. There are numerous questions which are vital to the commercial life of the concern, where these interests have to be reconciled and the integrated decision expressed as a definite part of the policy of the undertaking. Frequently they are answered as the result of traditional practice or guess-work. Sometimes there is no decision at all. The business simply follows the market.

But it is increasingly evident that business decisions if they are to be effective must be based upon facts. While a selling department can accumulate valuable and essential facts, its opinions are apt to be biassed by the special nature and requirements of its own work. Moreover, its facts are what the retailer said to the wholesaler who repeated it to the Area Manager who told the Sales Manager who talked to the Production Director. There must be effective arrangements for market research if direct and accurate knowledge of the needs of consumers is to be the basis of activity. Only so can a whole series of questions which affect both the producer and the distributor be dealt with satisfactorily.

Efforts on the part of the manufacturer will, however, be largely ineffective unless the distributor plays his part. There is at the moment a great deal of criticism based on the growing " spread " between the ex-factory cost of goods and the final cost to the consumer. Many attempts are being made to analyse the actual costs of distribution. A modern distributing business cannot be managed successfully without proper cost analysis of all phases of operation. On the other hand, figures showing that a business with a certain turnover costs rather more to run per £ of sales than another business of a smaller size, are not evidence of lack of efficiency. What really makes the difference in price to the consumer is whether the distributor's orders are put to the manufacturer in a shape which will enable him to get the full economies possible with machine production. It is this which will make the closer linking together of consumers and distributors so profitable.

Any general charge of inefficiency levied against distributors as a body is manifestly unreasonable. Many modern distributive enterprises, such as the best of the great department stores and multiple shops, have devoted an attention to the scientific study of their problems of internal administration quite as intensive and pervasive as that developed by the most noteworthy productive enterprises. The fact that retailers serving different areas are not in direct competition one with another has greatly facilitated a free exchange of information as to management practices. Such comparison of figures and methods is the surest stimulus for the individual enterprise towards a higher standard of achievement. Thus in the United States a number of large department stores were the first to set up a properly organised group for research into their management practices—the Retail Research Association. Similarly in the international field a number of department stores in various countries have again been the first to establish the International Association of Department Stores.

But such studies by the leading and most progressive undertakings by no means cover the whole field of distributive activities. Moreover, improvements in the internal administration of distributive enterprises do not necessarily touch directly upon the vital point which is the basis of the argument developed in this chapter. They do not necessarily co-ordinate the efforts of the two interests *at the point of junction.*

Generally speaking, it is not untrue to say that distributors as a body have as yet shown little appreciation of the fundamental principles which have created modern productive capacity.   Nor is this a matter for surprise.   Those principles have issued from the discipline of a machine technology based on the exact sciences to which the manufacturer has been exposed for more than a century. The distributor on the contrary is perpetually under the direct influence of the consumer.   And, for reasons given in the first chapter of this section, consumer demand has shown a tendency to become increasingly erratic, variable and unpredictable. It is the distributor's task to offer to the public both novelty and variety, variety in quality, in pattern, in size and in range.   If he cannot do this he is an unsuccessful retailer.

Stated summarily, the fundamental principles of modern machine production are simplification and standardisation, applied both to products and to processes, leading to systematic planning of manufacturing operations designed to secure the maximum utilisation of mechanical equipment. This involves the longest possible machine runs on one pattern or process uninterrupted by the necessity of changing over to other patterns or processes.

The distributor can, if he will, do much to adapt his practices so that they accord with the conditions under which the manufacturer must work if he is to offer goods at the minimum possible price.   He can in his sphere simplify, standardise, plan and cost.   He can be of immense assistance to his suppliers.   Nor does this apply only to those special forms of distributive undertaking which are designed to provide a mass outlet for the products of mass production and which were touched upon in the preceding chapter.

One leading retailer engaged in the department store field has written :

> " Production is becoming more and more planned. Do we ever plan distribution ? Production is being progressively simplified. It reduces the number of patterns ; it makes the same parts do for several patterns. Do distributors simplify ? Production is more and more closely controlled ; do we control our buyers ? " [1]

Out of those questions he came to a very simple conclusion. " Everybody said to me, you cannot plan distribution, you depend on the customer. Fashion changes him almost every day ; he always wants the thing you have not got, and so on. We set to work to plan distribution, simplifying first." He set to work to plan distribution by simplifying his stock. If a man is keeping a shop for a certain class of customer and he has an incomplete range of sizes or of patterns of a particular article on his shelves, he is keeping a bad shop. He cannot simplify on patterns or sizes unduly because he is a retailer, and it is his job to buy for the needs of the public. But the retailer can simplify on price.

He can make up his mind that for each article he stocks he will not have more than three retail prices, that is three qualities to sell at retail. This plan has been tried over a number of years and has been successful. Every shop has, after all, a fairly definite clientele from the point of view of social classes. Mrs. A. when she goes to buy a

[1] Cf. E. A. Filene, *The Model Stock Plan*, New York, 1930.

hat, buys a hat for everyday ; sometimes she feels extravagant and buys a plus hat. Mrs. B. is in the next income class above Mrs. A. She does just the same, but her everyday hat is Mrs. A.'s plus hat and her extravagance is a plus-plus hat. Generally speaking for almost every article there are these three prices—the everyday price for bottom income groups, a middle price representing a " best " purchase for the bottom income groups and everyday for the higher incomes, and a top price representing the " best " purchase for the higher incomes. The whole of the stock of the department store in question was simplified on that basis. From that flowed other elements in planning.

The buyers found one of the factors of uncertainty eliminated from their work and their relations with suppliers. They were no longer trying to compare three variables, price, quality and pattern. They had only got to get the best quality on the market in any line to sell at a definite price. In the second place bargains were specialised. Bargains, which are goods which can be sold below cost, usually arise from a manufacturing or distributive misfortune : they should not be repeated. Bargains were sold in a basement on the strict understanding that they could not be repeated and must be sold within a limited period. The regular buyers were not always after " bargains ". Having a definite price to which to buy they could collaborate with suppliers far more closely.

In nine cases out of ten the normal retail

establishment, if it will take the trouble to do the research, will find that there are two or three standard prices for each article at which the great mass of its customers are prepared to buy and to buy freely. If then, its buyers are instructed to buy to those prices, allowing for a normal margin of gross profit, one variable in their relations with suppliers is eliminated. The supplier knows that his job is to offer the maximum possible value at that price. The buyer knows that where a particularly desirable article does not come within his price, he can probably get it there by offering a quantity order. The whole relationship is changed from one of a bargain to one of a mutual effort to meet the consumer. Incidentally the manufacturer has a tremendous stimulus to efficiency.

Another direction in which the distributor can help the manufacturer is in relation to the study of the laws which govern price. A famous department store in New York records an interesting experiment in the effect of price on demand. They had a stock of ingenious and attractive electric lamps retailing at $9. As the depression deepened they reduced to $8 . . . no result, then to $7 . . . no result, then to $6.50, and suddenly they couldn't get enough deliveries from the manufacturer to meet the demand. Later, when a brisk but stabilised sale at $6.50 had been running for some months, they tried reducing to $6 . . . no increase, and again to $5.50 . . . no increase. So they went back to $6.50 and the sales held. Obviously there was for that article a " critical " price at which it would sell freely. Now that information was of vital moment to the manufacturer. He should have this sort of detailed knowledge about every one of his products. But he can only get it if he and the various distributive agencies through which he is working are collaborating closely.

What is business going to do about this situation ? Is it going to allow these forces to work themselves out blindly, till the community through the state is forced to intervene for the sake of common order and decency ? Is it, in the field of distribution, going to repeat the disgusting hardships, the blindness to human values, which under a false conception of " economic law ", god-fearing and conscientious employers allowed themselves to tolerate in the middle decades of the nineteenth century ? Are business men going to wait till shops acts, selling acts, advertising acts have to be added to Factory Acts, to force them to realise that the principle of self-interest has limits, limits immutably founded in the fact of their mutual interdependence ?

# VIII

## " £5,000,000 LOST.

The affairs of the English Steel Corporation were mentioned in the Chancery Division today when Mr. Justice Bennett confirmed a scheme to reduce the capital of the Corporation from £8,234,889 to £2,862,069. Mr. Gordon Brown for the Corporation said the basis on which an amalgamation had been made in 1929 had turned out to be altogether too hopeful.

Mr. Justice Bennett : ' It has made a loss of £5,000,000 in three years.'

Mr. Brown : ' I would hardly call it a loss. This is rather a revaluation of assets.'

' But the scheme didn't work ? '

' No, it didn't work.'

' Is that rationalisation of industry ? ' asked the Judge amid laughter. Later he enquired : ' What exactly does rationalisation mean ? '

Mr. Brown said it was a word which originated in Parliament to mean amalgamation."—*Daily Paper.*

## CHAPTER VIII

### THE RATIONALISATION OF DISTRIBUTION

WHERE ignorance is wit it is perhaps folly to be wise. When the representative of a great Corporation declares in open Court that rationalisation was " a word which originated in Parliament to mean amalgamation," it is not surprising that the general public should be prepared to laugh about it. If rationalisation meant amalgamation, that and nothing else, there was no point in inventing a new word to describe an old phenomenon. In fact, it was an unpardonable waste of parliamentary time. All that is needed for recovery is a united effort to revive the Frothblowers. Their motto was, " The more we are together, the merrier we'll be." Indeed in the light of this extract a second line might be added —" The Lord is my receiver, when broke in company." To set half a dozen bankrupt businesses to keep house together offers no security to their creditors.

But of course rationalisation means much more than that. Merely to amalgamate offers an opportunity for rationalisation. It may remove some of the difficulties which stand in the way of rationalisation—nothing more. Indeed, if the amalgamation has not in itself been rational, has not fitted together enterprises which technically and economically belong together and will really gain in ability to serve the consumer by unifying their control, amalgamation may well set up obstacles to true rationalisation.

Rationalisation is not a method or a system : it is a state of mind. In the first place it does not accept the profit of the individual enterprise as the final criterion of social usefulness. On the other hand it does not necessarily call the profit-motive into question.

" The profit motive, whatever may be said against it, has proved dependable, steady, always on the job. . . . Such a dependable motive power as this is surely worth considering. If it can be attached to a machine well designed to serve the common welfare, the common welfare would seem to be assured, whereas if the common welfare is dependent upon keeping idealism at white heat there is no such assurance." [1]

Rationalisation does suggest that profit does not provide a complete and final measure by which to judge economic arrangements. It provides some criterion. Profit there must be in the sense that the community is prepared to pay as much for the service as the service costs, plus as much as will keep that service at the maximum pitch of efficiency by constantly renewing its equipment and enabling it to raise the money required for development. Without that sort of yardstick efficiency is impos-

[1] E. A. Filene, *Successful Living in this Machine Age*, London : Jonathan Cape.

sible. Russia has discovered this. Communists speak of " insisting on a business system of accounting " : in other words economic enterprises must relate expenditure to income. But, because a particular business arrangement is profitable to an individual over the period which happens to suit his convenience, that is not final evidence of its utility to the community.

When the XYZ Dubious Finance Corporation Ltd. floats a heavy issue of shares on a necessarily large volume of water—the larger the bucket-shop the more often it goes to the well—the transaction is apt to be of no value to anyone, except the Directors of the Corporation. That they have made a profit, is no criterion of the worth of the arrangement. Similarly where shareholders insist on dividing paper profits up to the hilt without adequate provision for material obsolescence or for maintaining the loyal service of the best quality of management, those who get out in time will reap a nice profit. But again this offers no criterion of the value of the arrangement to the rest of the world.

Rationalisation does insist on such a criterion . . . not an ideal reference to the " rights of man, or equal pay for equal work, or art for party's sake " or any phrase . . . but a perfectly plain economic yardstick by which to judge economic arrangements . . . the principle of least waste. Before every job, every system, every bit of organisation it puts this interrogation : " Is this, from the standpoint of the community as a whole, the least wasteful way of getting this piece of work done ?

Does it involve the minimum use of both material and of human effort ? "

The question is not, is this the least wasteful method of getting the work done which will also suit Tom's or Dick's or Harry's personal convenience ? Tom may want to buy a new motorcar this year, and a 15 per cent. dividend will suit him nicely. Dick is getting too old to take as active a part in the business as he used to do : but, the Managing Director's salary doesn't go as far as it did, and this new treatment for rheumatism is so expensive. " That young chap whom Harry's second daughter married last autumn, he is a bit of an ass, but one's son-in-law, damn it, and the girl's just going to have a baby."

That is all very human and natural. But it is not rationalisation. It is not sound economics. And because those in a position to do these things rather like doing them, that is no reason for attempting to disguise them as principles. They are in fact a mild form of falsifying accounts. The 15 per cent. dividend that hasn't really been earned should be labelled " to private car for Sales Director ". The chance of a suitable amalgamation lost because Dick didn't want to retire should be shown as " loss due to lack of pension scheme ", or alternatively, thinking of his rheumatism, " insurance for office boy." The fact that the concern has a second-rate engineer where it might have had a first-class man cheaper, should appear as " Maternity benefit for Production Director's daughter ".

Rationalisation establishes the criterion of least waste as the basis for passing on all economic arrangements—the mark to be aimed at. In the second place it carries the intellectual method, the mental attitude of the scientific management engineer outside the bounds of the individual business. It suggests that in determining how business is to be carried on with least waste every single activity and relationship should be examined from the scientific standpoint. There should be brought to bear upon them every atom of exact knowledge, every device of statistical or other forms of measurement, every refinement of analysis that can be discovered or devised. It suggests in short that decisions should be based not on opinion, or guess-work or tradition or habit, but on facts, and, moreover, that business should be unwearying in testing and assaying the facts it has and in the search for new facts bearing upon the situation.

Science has little time for patent medicines. It prefers the slower and infinitely more laborious process of discovering the laws of health. Hitherto the main law of economic health on which the world has concentrated has been the principle that all should produce as much and as cheaply as possible. Under these conditions there will be more to exchange, more to go round. The assumption has been that the economic order was a " natural order ", that money and goods would circulate naturally like the blood stream in a physical body, that the individual's desire for gain and the force of competition would interact inevitably to secure effective distribution. That, obviously, has not happened. There is no apparent reason why it should. The activities which constitute the structure of distributive action, the payment of wages and dividends, the engagement of salesmen, the setting up of wholesale, retail and transport businesses, etc. etc., depend, each of them, on human, individual, would-be-reasonable decisions. There is no warrant for assuming that the sum of those individual decisions will issue in the most economical arrangements for distribution unless each trader has an exact and scientific knowledge of all the actions and reactions which will result from what he decides to do.

But, as a consequence of this assumption, men have expended money and energy in no small measure in the scientific study of production, while they have spent almost no money on the scientific study of distribution. Above all, scientific method has not been fully applied at the point of junction between those engaged in production and those engaged in distribution, and this, as has been shown, is the critical point. It is true in general that the more there is produced the more there is to exchange. It ceases to be true if traders produce either the wrong sort of things so that no one wants to buy them, or produce them at the wrong price to the consumer so that they cannot be sold, or if the earnings of those engaged in production are so reduced that they cannot buy even if they would.

In short on all that series of problems concerned

with price, and range, and packing and presentation and speed of turnover which are described as marketing problems, there has been far less definite research than in the field of production. Great Britain has had for over a decade a Department of Scientific and Industrial Research supported by public funds and occupied with the chemical and physical problems of the materials and processes of manufacture. Much more recently it established an Empire Marketing Board. That institution was the first public department which the May Committee selected for the exercise of economy. It has now been destroyed despite a strong public opinion in favour of maintaining it.

In the previous chapters dealing with Distribution this position has been reviewed from the standpoint of the individual manufacturer, his need for a separate marketing department and for market research, and from the standpoint of the relations between individual manufacturer and individual distributor. But, it is clear that the individual manufacturer or distributor cannot command, working alone and single-handed, all the information they require to come to sound conclusions as to their markets. Further than this, there are other points, where it is essential that they should act in common with others in like case not only to get information, but to determine and to give effect to a sound policy for the industry and for the trade to which they belong. If the point of junction between producer and distributor is the critical point in our economic situation, it is a point which can only be attacked by producers and distributors acting in collaboration as organised bodies.

In the first volume of his *History of the British Army* the Hon. J. W. Fortescue, in discussing army organisation during the War of the Spanish Succession, wrote :

" Englishmen have ever had a passion for independent command. To this day (1899), as the history of the volunteers shows, there are many men who, though unwilling to serve in any existing corps, would cheerfully expend ten times the care, trouble, and expense on a regiment, or even on a troop or company of their own."

What Fortescue wrote of the Englishman of 1899 and of the early eighteenth century is still true to-day. But England is another thirty-four years into the evolution of machine production. Machines spell division of labour, specialisation. And the corollary of specialisation is co-ordination. Machines too have a nasty habit of refusing to recognise national peculiarities. There is a story of an English mechanic who " spoke to " a Ford : then he kicked it in the radiator. After that he decided to look under the bonnet and to adjust the distributor. After that the Ford consented to go.

Those who wish to live on terms with a machine age must risk some degree of co-ordination. But since tendencies of a national type are facts with which scientific examination has to deal, it may perhaps prove that where co-ordination is necessary, the best and most workable type of association, of relationship, between business units of predominantly Anglo-Saxon origin, is not the outright merger or even the detailed legal arrangement. Some looser form of gentlemen's agreement to do that which is of use to the trade or industry to which individual undertakings belong and to refrain from doing that which is hurtful to such common interests may serve the same purpose.

The primary fact which every trader ought to know in seeking to market any product is the total purchasing power of the market—the total part of the Income of all potential consumers which is available for retail purchases. He will want to know too how that purchasing power is distributed. Such distribution takes three forms. There is distribution by area, the purchasing power per head of the population varying in different areas. Then there is distribution by social groups : there is the £1,000 a year group and the poverty line group : there is the married group and the single group : there is the group with children and without : there is grouping by sex, by age, by profession and so on. All these facts affect purchasing habits. Finally, and this is the most important distinction of all, there is commodity grouping. He will want to know what proportion of expenditure in various groups is, as it were, earmarked for the primary necessities of food, clothing and shelter, and what proportion is optional.

One research worker, seeking for market information in Great Britain, has described how he tried " to see what there was of use *concealed* in official records ",[1] and how finally in 1929 the results of the 1924 Census of Production were published. That "concealed" is very much to the point : and as for the 1924 Census of Production the detailed results for one of the most critical industries, cotton textiles, appeared in 1930.

The individual manufacturer or trader working alone cannot get adequate statistics of purchasing power, its distribution and use. As long as he acts individually he must just take what is handed out to him when and where he can find it, like a child at a "hunt the treasure" party. Nor has he one atom of right to criticise the Government or the civil service. He is only in process of becoming distribution and consumer conscious himself. He cannot expect the government departments concerned to appreciate his need unless he formulates it and insists on its being met, in an organised way.

Compare the situation in Great Britain with regard to production. In modern business adequate and up-to-date statistics of consumption and purchasing power are essential tools in effective marketing. In the first place, what manufacturer requiring a special variety of steel for his tool-room work would consent for two minutes "to see what there was of use concealed in his suppliers' catalogues"? In the second place, he would have no need to do so. A brief enquiry to the National Physical Laboratory, one of the finest of its kind

[1] H. Weeks, M.A., in an address on Market Research given at the Central Hall, Westminster, April 20th, 1932.

in the world, would tell him immediately if there was any official information on the point. If there wasn't and it was, as is the case with consumption statistics, a matter of general interest to his trade, he would be able to apply to his Trade Research Association for information and possibly for a special investigation. Whatever imperfections have yet to be overcome, on the production side, there is definite machinery organised at two levels, nationally and by industries, to give the essential facts.

On the distribution side the machinery is haphazard. As a result of the old diplomatic tradition and a growing interest in imperial economic collaboration, there has been some national effort with regard to export markets—a Department of Overseas Trade and an Empire Marketing Board. But the domestic market is of equal and growing importance. Here there is practically nothing. This situation will continue until business men in their organised capacity—at both levels, both by trades and nationally—insist that official statistics should be published in the form in which they are needed in time to be of practical use.

The United States in 1930 completed for the first time in the history of any industrialised country a complete national census of distribution. Preliminary figures were available in the first half of 1931 and the final reports were practically completed by December 1932. Her traders have thus a complete survey of the whole of the distributive mechanism of the country. They know the number of retail and wholesale establishments by kinds, by size and by type of organisation in each area and in each trade. They have figures as to their turnover and most of the principal items in distributive cost. They have less complete, but very enlightening information as to their trade by various commodity groups. Similarly they have available for each manufacturing industry an analysis of the different channels through which its products are distributed and the volume passing through each channel. Industry in all countries depends on a well-organised and assured domestic market as a foundation for efficient mechanical production. It is a matter for discussion whether, putting the interest of the community aside, traders in other countries can afford to allow the greatest potential competitor in the world to remain alone in command of the immense advantages conferred by such a complete and analytic knowledge of its domestic distribution.[1]

In regard to export markets the individual trader who tries to walk by himself is equally handicapped in obtaining the information necessary to a scientific attack on his problems. Where distant and foreign countries are concerned, the reports of agents or salesmen are an inadequate index of economic and political conditions. They reflect

[1] For a fuller account of the American Census, vide *The United States Census of Distribution*, 1930, a Report issued by The International Management Institute on behalf of The International Distribution Commission, Geneva, 1933.

the mood of the moment as reports from men of similar status on the domestic market would do.

The annual reports of the Department of Overseas Trade are the best general documents available in Great Britain. They are written sometimes in officialese, and are bound, as are many Government documents, in a format which exclaims : " Please don't read me ; I'm dull." But they are accurate. And a knowledge of their contents is essential as a background against which the more frequent news of the daily and weekly Press can be interpreted correctly. Manufacturers should use the Department in season and out of season. A nation does not always get the Government it deserves ; but a business community always gets the service from official departments which it deserves. It should be remembered that correspondence in a Government office starts at the bottom and works up : the lower ranks look for precedents ; the seniors have to take decisions.

There is a story of an unemployed man who was a little truculent at a Labour Exchange. The official in charge said : " Do you know who you are talking to ? " The man replied : " 'Course I do. I'm talking to my paid servant. Just remember this : if there were no unemployed my side the counter, you wouldn't be sitting on that stool." Business is too apt to forget that a civil servant is, as his title implies, an employee of the public. He is there to render a service. Public money is being wasted unless there is effective collaboration between the official and private agencies interested in business. The traditional attitude of business towards the state of " go and see what Tommy's doing and tell him not to " is inappropriate to modern conditions. It should be changed to " go and see what Tommy's doing and help him to do it better ". The initiative in recent years has come too largely from the Government side. Traders should use and, if necessary, abuse Government agencies ; but, above all, they should take the trouble to be interested in their actions.

In conclusion, on this point, it may be noted that no market is worth trading in which the chief does not think is worth a personal visit at fairly frequent intervals. If a market is too small for this it becomes an immediate case for examination as to the possibilities of combined trading by the industry.

Action, however, to develop information which is limited to that obtainable from central official sources will be unbalanced. Much can be done to further a scientific approach to questions of distribution by combined action on the part of traders themselves. Such combined action may be of many kinds and based on various principles of association. There is in the U.S.A. a very successful little group of ten firms who sell various different products to stationery retailers. They have learned a very great deal about their distributive problems by studying them in conjunction over two or three years. Consumer surveys for individual producers are probably best carried out by a competent advertising agency. A modern advertising agency must know more about its own highly specialised trade than any single manufacturer or trader can know. It will know still more if it has a qualified and modern research department.

But advertising agents are themselves individual traders. Probably 25 per cent. of the time of their research departments is at present expended on accumulating statistical information, and particularly information bearing on press circulation which is of general interest to business and not special to the needs of a particular client. One agency known to the author has some admirable shaded maps indicating at a glance the exact circulation covered throughout the British Isles by an advertisement placed in each of the leading dailies separately, and again in various combinations of dailies. The agency in question is dealing at the outside with 1 per cent. to 3 per cent. of the press advertising of the country. Its careful, ingenious, scientific work is of general interest and utility and steps should be taken to make it generally available.

The manufacturer or trader who wishes to advertise effectively cannot walk alone. He should employ a first-class agent. But equally the agent should not walk alone. He cannot serve his clients to his maximum capacity or give them adequate information as to media, unless he is co-operating closely with other agents with a view to strengthening and perfecting their mutual professional service by exchanging every scrap of information of a general character which does not betray the confidence of a particular client. There is at present great waste in the advertising world for lack of a properly financed central research agency, supported by the whole profession, which would pool all information of this general type.

With regard to the dislocating effect of " the new competition "—competition from alternative means of expenditure rather than from other manufacturers of the same or similar articles—group advertising is a possible solution. It is the cheapest form of publicity at present available in many industries. Competitive advertising within an industry frequently only stabilises the sales of the different undertakings one as against another at an unnecessarily low level in total. The main function of advertising today is to create new markets, not to fight over the carcase of old markets.

National statistics need to be supplemented by local statistics. There is need for information on local buying power and numbers of selling points. Today Great Britain is dependent for most of its knowledge in such matters on a decennial census of the population. Regional surveys have been conducted here and there, as in the Liverpool and Cardiff areas. But there must be concealed in the administrative records of local government far more detailed and timely information on both these points. Business on the other hand has its own regional organisation in the local chambers of commerce : these are again linked nationally into the Association of British Chambers of Commerce. These bodies might with advantage devote more attention to collaboration with local authorities in the issue of periodic and accurate information as to the industrial and commercial structure of their localities. Here again the individual trader is practically helpless. He is inevitably suspected of seeking some special advantage for himself. Acting in collaboration, as the business community, he can achieve an immense amount with little more outlay than at present.

General statistics require working upon and specialising for the needs of particular trades. That should be the function of the Trade Associations. These bodies, because of their dependence upon industry and their more intimate contact with it, can obtain more refined and confidential figures than are ever available to public authorities. A well-run Trade Association should be a goldmine of vital information. But many Secretaries of Trade Associations are not primarily interested in statistics. They are admirable lawyers or accountants. But the statistical insight necessary to hammer out a wise policy for their industry is often missing. Yet that is their primary function.

This is certainly work which the manufacturer cannot do alone. It is work which the Trade Association should not seek to do in isolation. It should be integrated with the general statistical work of the public departments, staffed and equipped to carry through this kind of technical activity. Business has its political organisations and its organisations for dealing with labour questions : these tasks have nothing to do either with politics or personnel. They are a scientific job—the linking of technical men, statisticians, research workers who labour in business, with their opposite numbers in the great public departments, on terms which will enable business as a whole to make good its requirements in the interests of the community.

This then is what is necessary for the rationalisation of distribution. There is needed an unremitting effort to build up new mechanisms of coordination, to adopt and modify those which exist already, so that they are fitted to discharge the wider functions which improvement in communications and in productive methods render utterly essential. At present the machinery of collaboration is inadequate and haphazard. There is much overlapping, waste and confusion of purpose, with consequent rivalries. This is not the fault of the officials of these institutions who are frequently energetic and devoted. But the situation will continue as long as business men regard voluntary associations as luxuries or trimmings.

Every industry in every country should have its Council representing consumers, distributors and producers in that trade. Every locality should have its Chamber dealing properly with regional business. Every nation should have its economic general staff assisting and collaborating with these subsidiary agencies in the general planning of its affairs and integrating its economic activities with those of other nations. These bodies should be created, not by the state alone, but by business itself acting in collaboration with the state : they should exist not to command, but to advise and to inform. Above all they should be adequately staffed.

Not only by great amalgamations, but by a change of outlook, not by force, but by knowledge, not by destroying individualism, but by educating it, will stability and prosperity return. It has been suggested that Rationalisation is a half-way house between *laisser-faire* and a controlled economy. It is not any fixed point. It is a way of progress— the road by which the world must travel from the ignorance and hazard of its present methods, to something more informed, more knowledgeable, more exact, and more secure—rather a self-controlled economy.

# PART FOUR

## TRAINING FOR MANAGEMENT

## IX

" It was universally supposed, for instance, that labour was a commodity. Nevertheless, labour could not and did not act like a commodity. It acted like human beings. It acted, in fact, from much the same motives with which employers acted, and not even the most dismal economist supposed that employers were commodities."—E. A. FILENE, *Successful Living in this Machine Age.*

" It has been borne in upon us time and again that our educational system is too remote from life. . . . An English humanism, including the study of literature, of history and of the language as an instrument of thought and expression, if made actual by being brought closely into touch with the main preoccupations of the students, might go far not only to ennoble the education of the industrial worker but also to bridge the gap between industry and culture."—*The Teaching of English in England,* Departmental Report, 1921.

# CHAPTER IX

## THE EDUCATION AND TRAINING OF FOREMEN
## AND SUPERVISORS

THE foreman or supervisor is already the somewhat bewildered subject of an enormous literature. But the writers of books for him and about him, seem to be agreed on one subject only—his vital importance in the industrial scheme of things. Sometimes he must feel a little like God in the hands of the theologians.

To write of the training of foremen without a minute analysis of the available books may appear presumptuous. There are " The Foreman and His Job " by X., " How we train Supervisors " by Y., and " Education for Foremanship " by Z., demy octavo 50 and 700 pages with 3 tables and 10 illustrations, $5 net or by our special instalment plan. But this literature has its dangers. The first is indigestion. Then there is the fallacy of " the practical man ". The subject is too wide to be confined to the narrow field of personal experience. It is misleading to discuss it from the angle of " How we train Foremen in the Blankshire Lemonjuice Co. Ltd.", with timetables of lectures and correlations all complete. There is no significance in autobiography of the cabin-boy to admiral persuasion, adorned with the chosen generalisations of the Managing Director who first learned the meaning of S.P.Q.R. at a foreman's study circle in Roman history. On this question business is only groping. All these attempts to work out a technique of foreman training, to collate existing experience, are premature. They lack any foundation in a clear vision of the aim.

This of course is true in part of any system of education. But it is particularly true of education designed for any grade of person engaged in industry. Machine industry is a very recent institution indeed. It is also a highly dynamic institution at a particularly active period of its evolution. And in all the questions which are concerned with management, with the relations between those grades in industry whose duty is to plan and to direct and those who co-operate with them, this dynamic characteristic is particularly marked. It is at an intensely interesting stage of development, a stage which has sometimes been called " the second industrial revolution ".

It is the inevitable handicap of almost all systems of education that they tend to prepare for the world as it was yesterday rather than for the world as it will be tomorrow. By the time living, vital, creative thought has become part of the general intellectual currency of mankind so that it can be netted in pedagogic expositions and compressed to the bare skeletons of textbook practice, it is almost always out of date. The vast bulk of vocational training is merely the inculcation of knowledge which has already lost touch with truth. What is true of all education, is, for the reasons given, doubly true of systems designed for those who work in industry.

It is impossible to design a suitable scheme of training for any office, any group of duties, unless the nature of that office, the requirements of those duties have first been determined. In the case of the positions of foremen and supervisors, this is not the case. As an example may be quoted the results of a job analysis of a medium-sized British factory employing about 7,000 people. There were some hundreds of so-called foremen. No two of their job analyses read the same. The term covered every grade and variety of duty and responsibility from posting wage-books to the management of a large and varied department. And what is true of that factory is, *mutatis mutandis*, true of every factory in Europe and of a large majority of those in the United States.

Two men in a given factory with ostensibly the same official degree of authority may and frequently do exercise in practice degrees of supervision that are psychologically poles asunder. It will take half a century at least for principles of authority to be worked out and to become established in the great body of industrial life. In the meanwhile the exercise of direction and control must remain haphazard and unco-ordinated.

Thus the terms " foreman " and " supervisor " cover a group of widely dissimilar positions, entirely lacking in any common or accepted principles, either as to the duties involved or as to the degree of authority implied and the nature of the sanctions supporting it. It is a reasonable assumption that there is only one element in these titles which is common to any large number of enterprises, namely, that they imply those individuals in the industrial hierarchy who are directly in touch with the great body of workers whether operative or clerical. That of course is an important fact. It gives some basis for discussion. But it is the sole fact to build upon. The quality and kind of relations which should subsist between the workers and those immediately in contact with them are undefinable. Because working relations must depend on the nature of the work. And here the dynamic character of industrial organisation steps in. No one knows what the character of the foreman's work is going to be, even a decade ahead.

The idea of applying the method of thought, the intellectual technique evolved by the scientists to the problems of industrial management is yet young. Taylor died, at a comparatively early age, in 1915. There has been little or no opportunity for genuine experiment on a conclusive scale with the more revolutionary and far-reaching of his ideas. Among these is the conception of functional foremanship. The idea underlying that conception was integral, an essential development of his whole industrial philosophy. The wider application of this cardinal principle of industrial organisation is an inevitable development. It will come slowly, but it will come none the less surely, probably within a few decades.

Taylor's analysis of the qualities and duties required of the foreman under the older form of industrial organisation is unanswerable. He listed nine qualities which the foreman was called upon to possess, including Brains, Education, Tact, Special Knowledge, Energy, Grit, Honesty, Judgment, and Good Health. It led directly to his conclusion that the job is an impossible one, that only one man in a thousand can be found who is really competent to fill it—and he is naturally not available at a foreman's wage. Taylor knew very little about experimental psychology. But his analysis was curiously confirmed by Mr. Ordway Tead whose *Instincts in Industry* contains a fascinating summary of the mental conflict involved in the traditional foreman's position.

In the second place, even since Taylor's time, the amount and range of specialised knowledge which should be employed in the everyday tasks of industrial management has increased enormously. In the case of the higher executive positions, it is probably unnecessary, even if it were possible, for the administrator to be intimately acquainted with all the sciences which bear on his task. He must delegate to and co-ordinate the work of experts. It is sometimes forgotten, especially in the discussion of educational schemes, that the foreman has no one to whom to delegate. The trend of industrial organisation must be similar to the general tendency of all the social organisation of our time—which is increasingly to confide work of all kinds to functional specialists. The foreman cannot be left out of this process, a relic of an older system, still a Jack of all Trades. Even a buffer will lose its resilience if it is hit too hard and too often.

Most important of all, the greater function-alisation of management, alone of all the theories of industrial organisation which have been put before us in the last decades, really goes to the heart of the question of the control of industry. Mr. H. G. Wells has written :

"A vast amount of moral force has been wasted in the past hundred years by the antagonism of Labour to Capital, as though this was the primary issue in human affairs. But this never was the primary issue and it is steadily receding from its former importance."

That is literally true. No man, whatever his political complexion, who has any practical experience of administration today, really pretends to himself that a mere shift of ownership in the means of production, or in the right to its surplus, will make any fundamental difference in industrial relations. Whatever the ownership of industry, the real hardships will continue unless there is a fundamental change in organisation and method.

Industrial unrest is something far more subtle than a vague sense of injustice which is open to legal adjustment. It is the expression of an objection to direction and obligation in themselves, become articulate with the spread of political liberty and popular education. And the sole valid answer to that objection is to show that direction and obligation are not personal, not enforced by sanctions which rest on might, but natural, inevitable in the order of things if the world is to be clothed and housed and fed. That is to say the answer to the workers' sense of grievance is exactly the same answer as Taylor gave, when challenged on the ground that his functional foremanship contravenes the principle that " no man can serve two masters ". He replied that it did not upset the principle, but enforced it. Under functional foremanship everyone, employer, foreman, and workers alike, serves one master . . . knowledge. Looked at in this way functional organisation contains the germ of a real hope, a permanent resolution of our discontents. For it envisages an industrial society in which all shall be both servants and masters each in their turn, masters in those things in which each has special knowledge and training, and servants in those things in which others are more instructed.

If evolution of industrial organisation in this direction is inevitable, for what duties are foremen and supervisors to be educated? Clearly existing methods will not do. What is wanted is a scheme of training designed to fit men and women for the duties of the foreman and supervisor as they will be tomorrow. They must be educated, not for what is, but for what will be.

If the term foreman or supervisor does imply an individual who, in some managerial capacity or other, is in direct contact with the worker, and within a decade or so the group of duties at present conventionally allotted to the foreman is likely to be broken down into a variety of more specialised tasks, these are at least indications of limitations. It is obviously hopeless to try to educate future foremen for all of the eight or ten special functions for any one of which they may be selected.

Any system of education for these positions, if it is to be of practical utility, must be largely confined to the one common element of contact with the workers. That is, the first quality of primary import which it should seek to develop in future foremen and supervisors is leadership. It should abandon any attempt to inculcate special knowledge of the various functions, any one of which he may be called upon to perform and none of which he can be taught thoroughly in the time available. Rather it should concentrate on that general attitude towards industrial work, that faculty of appreciating the method and the spirit by which a number of specialised tasks may be united in furthering a single end, which is called co-operation. Leadership and co-operation—these are the two, and the only two, ends of importance towards which systems of foreman education should be directed.

It may be argued, that these are not intellectual attainments at all, things which can be taught. They are moral qualities, matters of the spirit. And it is doubtful if there is any system of training which will develop them.

This is, of course, in part true. It constitutes

the second main difficulty with the existing systems of foreman training. In nearly every instance when they speak of foremen or supervisors, they mean men and women who have already reached positions of minor responsibility in industry. It would be the grossest injustice to criticise as individuals, the noble and honourable workers who, with little opportunity, no immediate training, and against immense difficulties, are holding these appointments in industry today. But in the majority of cases, and more particularly in the older countries, where employment with the same concern is more stable and promotion less flexible than in the United States, the administration is starting to educate men and women when they are often of middle age, settled in their main characteristics, and liable to view with resentment any suggestion that they should go to school again. Management must help them all it can. It is its duty to do so. It is not their fault if they are unequal to the task and unsuitable material for instruction. But it should be recognised that any attempts in this direction are not systems of education at all. They are the veriest patchwork, making good at fifth best, the careless and short-sighted management of the past.

The majority of the foremen and supervisors in industry today have been selected, not for their possession of those qualities which have been indicated as important, but on one ground and one ground only—skill in the particular task which is to be supervised. Curiously enough, the great body of the workers seems to give a kind of tacit approval to this method. It seems natural to them that it should form the basis of selection. Yet it is as reasonable as selecting a corps of officers for an army on the basis of individual excellence at drill.

From this follows a further main conclusion. Any genuine system of training to equip foremen and supervisors must be a long-period system—a system designed for men and women who are selected when they are young, just because they show evidence of the possession of those qualities which have been indicated as essential.

There is a third difficulty with the majority of the systems of foreman training which have hitherto been described. They hail from the United States. European business men should be profoundly grateful to America for the quantity and quality of the original and courageous research which she is putting into these industrial problems. They cannot hope to better it. It is an inspiration and an encouragement. But on this subject, while it is immensely helpful and suggestive, it is inapplicable directly to European conditions.

The two qualities of leadership and co-operation are essentially personal attitudes towards two sets of industrial relationships. Subjectively they imply the power to inspire and to direct others on the one hand, and the power to work collectively with colleagues on the other, towards the fulfilment of a given task. Objectively they imply on the one hand the recognition of exceptional qualities which induce acceptance of direction, and on the other understanding of the common plan, and enthusiasm that others should have the fullest opportunity of making their maximum contribution to it.

Personal attitudes of this type are conditioned and determined largely by the social and group background against which individuals are set. It is not logic, but tradition and habit which guide individual action. There is a real and vital difference between the two continents in social background, particularly as it bears on this problem. The United States are a country which not only started with the constitutional assumption that all men are born free and equal, but a country where, owing to its physical break with the past and the rapid development of an almost virgin continent, men really do feel equal. Of course there are qualifications. It is said that you cannot convict a million dollars. It is unlikely that the Daughters of the Revolution would define liberty agreeably to John Stuart Mill. But there is a radical difference—a difference clear to every sensitive European the first time he asks for a shoeshine in New York. The American shoulders his knapsack with a baton swing so to speak. He " guesses " he may be President some day.

It is wholly significant that " guess ". In Europe people don't " guess ", except about horses. About the big social issues their attitude is one of knowing. The worker either " knows his place ", or he is convinced that it is only the bloodsucking capitalist who keeps him from what he " knows to be his rightful place ". Europe is still under the shadow of feudalism. Business men say, " I don't know what to do with my business when I die. You see I lost my boy in the war ". One wonders sometimes what they think their boys died for. There are parishes all up and down Europe where the parson and the squire still dominate the social situation. The long slow emancipation with its deep-set habits of mind and its crude reactions is still only in the making. But the United States put a knife through that tangle at Yorktown and the last litter was cleared away by the men who died at Gettysburg.

The difference is never clearer than in this question of foremanship. A foreman in the United States is a man who does a particular job. A foreman in Europe is still a man of a particular social class. That is why the American literature on foremanship is inapplicable to European conditions. What is more, it is apt to have a narcotic effect—to inhibit European employers from thinking through the situation honestly.

Co-operation is a state of mind. Men can be taught to co-operate on one basis and one basis only, enthusiasm for a common object which they understand and appreciate. The relations between the foreman and his employer in Great Britain are still almost invariably master-servant relations. The foreman is expected to co-operate as a matter of course, because he is a member of the staff. Employers who fully accept Trade Unionism as a reasonable economic device, of value to all concerned, go pale with rage and astonishment when members of their staff show any signs of group consciousness. But the economic relationship of the salaried staff, to the employer or owner group is precisely the same as the workers'. The staff are dismissed a little less easily, carried a little longer in times of adversity, because they cost more to replace. But that is their sole advantage. They are workers and wage earners all the same.

Why then does the employer get angry? Because he is still thinking in feudal terms. He would regard group action by his staff in defence of their economic position as " disloyalty to him ". And, generally speaking, the staff accept this view for much the same reasons. They have a position of privilege which carries certain social dignities. They are intensely class-conscious : they would sooner lose every hope of heaven than " come down in the world ". But the relation scarcely differs one iota from that between the baron and the crowd of understrappers, bailiffs, vintners, and what not who hung about the mediæval manor.

No common idea is put before men which can win their allegiance. It is moonshine to talk about co-operation with the workers, or to attempt to teach co-operation to foremen, unless and until the basis of that co-operation, its object, has been defined in terms which go beyond personal advantage and the individual dominance of the bandit chief, to a logical description of economic process as the servant of the community fit to command the willing adherence of thinking and civilised men. That must be the basis of all reasonable foremen training in co-operation—a statement of policy, the policy of the enterprise, which will hold water, which, in a phrase, will convince them that they " are in business for their health ".

This leads immediately to a second consideration. Some modification is needed in the conception of competition placed before those holding subordinate positions in business. Competition is a device with certain valuable applications to economic life. But in its crude form, " every man for himself and the devil take the hindmost " . . . it cannot be reconciled with the realities of modern industrial practice. These involve a technique of production which for its efficient working requires the most delicate co-ordination of countless specialised functions and processes in ever-increasing units of control. It calls for a degree of mutual understanding and forbearance, of appreciation of the other fellow's job, unparalleled in any other enterprise in human history.

In training the foreman of the future in co-operation the second main consideration is a course in economics which is practical and realistic, which puts competition in its place as a device of utility between groups of producers subject to certain controls which are in process of being worked out, a device which in the form of friendly emulation may be a useful stimulus to individuals or groups, but a device which otherwise has no place within the enterprise. As long as competition is treated as a basic principle of economic life, an end in itself, a guide to conduct, so long will the mental attitude and conduct of those who should be co-operating in industrial enterprises reflect that erosive belief.

Successful co-operation between human beings is primarily a question of successful communication. The Filene-Finlay simultaneous translation device which is being worked out experimentally at Geneva may well have a more profound influence on international relations than all the diplomats have had for a century. But communication between man and man is largely carried on by the written and spoken word, and even where men nominally speak the same language, words are tricky things. Training in self-expression is part of training in co-operation. A foreman's course in co-operation should certainly include what Mrs. Malaprop called "the nice derangement of epitaphs".

Second to facility of communication comes knowledge of what the other man's work signifies. Here again it is not a question of teaching details. It is impossible to train every foreman in costing, and personnel work, and chemistry and engineering and safety devices and a dozen other functions. Nor should it be attempted. What can be taught is the part each of these activities plays in the total effort of the concern—in short the elements of industrial organisation.

But both these last subjects are of infinitely less importance than the first two, which are not really academic subjects at all, but attitudes on the part of the employer. Only a revision of mental outlook on these questions can hope to resolve the acute conflict which the foreman's present position involves. The general object of the enterprise must be defined in terms which will enable him to feel an intelligent interest in its success on grounds of citizenship, not of personal adherence. His own position and the position of his group in the general structure of economic life should be expressed in a form which will neither damage his own instinctive loyalties to his worker colleagues from whose ranks he has come, nor his new loyalties to the management group.

It is worth noting that despite the lack of any basic conceptions consistent with the facts patent to the commonest observation, the manager and employer groups have managed, at least as far as Great Britain is concerned, to evoke an amazing degree of co-operative effort and of feeling for the concern as a concern from the lower grades of the staff. They should take no credit for it. It is merely a demonstration of the amazing susceptibility of the human mind to group loyalties and ideals—an almost untilled field in psychology. This one fact contains a core of hope for the future social progress of humanity.

Leadership remains for consideration. It has already been suggested that the foreman of the future can only be trained if he is caught young. But there is a further question. Leadership is a reciprocal relation. On the part of the leader it is an attitude compounded of self-confidence—

desire to take a lead, to initiate—and of sympathy for and understanding of those under his authority. On the part of the led it postulates absence of the desire for self-assertion, confidence in and affection for the leader, and that acceptance of his position which is usually described by saying that he possesses prestige. If it is true that to a large degree the old feudal habits of mind still persist in business life, it is at least arguable that such a relationship cannot be developed at its best in any system which draws the leader direct from the ranks of his fellows.

Business is desperately short of any real experience in this problem. It is only just beginning to realise that the modern large-scale business is a system of administration, rather than a glorified family party. But there are organisations which have been forced by their character deliberately to train to leadership. The army is one. Now it is nearly universal in the armies of the world to find this job of the leadership of small groups divided as it were into two functions. Consider the duties corresponding to the foreman's job, the small unit of command. In the British Army the minor unit of command is the Platoon. It has first of all a platoon officer, a man who is not usually drawn directly from the ranks, and never, except in emergency, from the ranks of the same regiment in which he serves as an officer. His job is essentially leadership—the moral part of the total task of commanding the platoon. Assisting him is a platoon sergeant, who, as it were, looks after the technical side of the work. He is expected to be able to manage men. He is usually an older man than his officer with a great deal more experience of the details of his profession. But he is not expected nearly to the same degree as the officer, to exercise that moral influence which is called leadership.

Turning back to industry it will be noted that the conventional foreman is promoted from the ranks in the same shop, largely because he is a good technical man. Sometimes he develops leadership, but how often? May not just here be the root of nine-tenths of the trouble which issues in strikes and bitterness, that there is no group in industry whose specific function it is to supply in close and intimate contact with the smaller units of control just those factors of prestige, of confidence and affection, which it is the express and defined task of the subaltern officer to evokè?

The Great War showed military training systems in operation on the largest possible scale. Organisations were expanded to twenty and thirty times their normal size with lightning rapidity, forced to train officers and non-commissioned officers in a twentieth part of the time usually considered desirable. That was a practical test of principles of organisation and command such as industry seldom contemplates. Yet, right up to the end of the war, young officers who were often silly, often lesser men than those they led, somehow or other gained an ascendancy which had nothing to do with courts martial and military discipline. So that their men loved them and laughed at them and would go through the fires of hell behind them.

It is a legitimate doubt, contemplating industry, with its muttering and disgruntled shops, its middle-aged foremen, often feared, sometimes respected, but seldom loved, whether it is possible to grow the flower of leadership in such a soil.

It will only be done if the men who are to supply the leadership factor in relation to the small groups of workers are specialised for this task to a far greater degree than is the case at present. It is doubtful if they can command sufficient prestige, at all events in the older countries, if they are put immediately in charge of men whose colleagues they were the day before yesterday. Above all they must stand or fall, as the officer in the army stands or falls, by the *morale* of their unit, by its general contentment and readiness to put forward co-operative effort.

This may seem to smack of inequality, of privileged classes. But there is one form of equality and one only which is of real value, and that is equality of opportunity. Undue sensitiveness about class is not confined to the more fortunate. And that is one of the greatest inhibitions from which business suffers when it tries to think scientifically about methods of administration. If a particular job requires that those who are going to hold it should be selected at an early age and carefully and specially trained for that service, that is a question of method, not of principle. The real gift of leadership is too rare and too precious for a community to refuse to use it wherever it is found and from whatever class it originates.

As to the subjects of training there are certain obvious points. No man is fully equipped to lead men in industry today who has not a working acquaintance with the findings of modern experimental psychology, and with fatigue study. He should too have some knowledge of modern labour movements and of Trade Union history.

But here again, as with co-operation, the vital lessons are a matter of attitude on the part of the employer or management. In the final reckoning the only school for leadership is to lead ; but to lead under sympathetic and careful direction. Every man who is qualifying for leadership should have the chance to make mistakes and to learn from them. He should learn too that leadership is not a matter of privilege, of titles and freedom from discipline, but of responsibility. Above all he should learn that men will follow only the man who puts their interests above his personal convenience.

Leadership can be taught. Here and there in isolated instances one finds examples of deliberate teaching in industry. But they are rare. This question needs thinking out again from the beginning. It is urgent. For until the problem is solved no changes in the higher organisation of industry will have much effect. In the long last it is the details of every day which count. Industrial relationships are made in the shops, in the intimate contacts with the workers in the smallest units of control and by those who represent to them personally and immediately the policies of the management.

In modern large-scale production there must be systems of administration and there must be discipline, whoever owns the capital, wherever the ultimate authority resides. No man or body of men taking over the control of English industry today would have any power whatever to alter the majority of the causes which underlie strikes and endemic discontent ; because the reciprocal relations between this key group of foremen and supervisors and the higher management group on the one hand, and the workers they supervise on the other, have never been worked out, the conceptions of authority and the methods by which it is enforced are alike feudal and elementary. There is no trained staff of small-group-leaders for the quite simple reason that the principles which should underlie such training have never been defined.

## X

" A classical training is admittedly productive of one great advantage over a training in science, and that is in the power it confers in *the balancing of probabilities in which the human element is dominant.* Science can make no provision for this, though of course history and modern literature can. Science has, however, one enormous advantage over all other subjects. All facts can be obtained at first hand and without resort to authority. The learner is thus put in the position of being able to reason with an entirely unprejudiced mind. It is this possibility of *self-elimination in forming a judgment* that must be regarded as the greatest possible specific result of scientific training."—F. W. WESTAWAY, *Scientific Method.*

" The man of affairs without science is like the physician who has fallen out of the anatomy and physiology he may once have known ; within limits he may be a shrewder and abler practitioner than an academic professor ; but this he will be at the cost of being stationary. . . . To principles sooner or later, the subtlest craftsman has to bow his head, or be left behind ; for, even while his hand is on his tools, by theory contingencies and complications are being detected and eliminated, and processes shortened and economised."
—T. E. ALLBUTT, *On Professional Education.*

# CHAPTER X

## THE EDUCATION OF THE ADMINISTRATOR

THE considerations examined in the previous chapters of this book all centre ultimately on two considerations. The tasks laid upon those responsible for the higher administration of business are increasingly complex. The community is vitally interested in their efficient discharge. The tempo of economic evolution, the speed of change both in method and in structure, have accelerated. It is inherently improbable that the attitudes and practices which were sufficient to secure the necessary supply of administrative capacity in the more leisurely conditions of the past will prove adequate to present and future needs.

When an individual business is expanding quickly the responsibilities of administration are both more exacting and call for a larger supply of men capable of sustaining them. This supply cannot be maintained if the advancement of able members of the staff has to wait upon a policy of identifying administrative office with inheritance of the ownership. Or at least it can only be maintained under such conditions if alternative opportunities, of salaried employment or of independent business venturing are few, and even then only with a considerable sacrifice of administrative efficiency. The normal age difference between two generations is from twenty-five to thirty years, too wide a gap in the continuity of administrative experience in a large-scale and growing concern.

The larger amalgamations of today do actually present to the administrator a series of problems differing in quality from any previously known to the business world. It is only within the last quarter of a century that units of more than 1,000 employees have been anything but an extreme rarity : previous to 1875 they were practically unknown. Competitive business is therefore very inexperienced in the handling of numbers larger than could be subjected to the direct personal influence of a dominating individual. Such experience as is available belongs to the domain of state administration and to the fighting services of the various governments. Business men themselves are frequently extremely critical about the efficiency of public administration. But it remains to be seen how far the special weaknesses to which public enterprises are proverbially subject, " red tape ", inter-departmental tribal warfare, inertia, refusal to take responsibility, bureaucracy, are really due to the absence of the money-making incentive, and how far they are merely a function of size, difficulties inseparable from all large-scale administration.

It is undeniable that where businesses have grown beyond the possibilities of individual control and insufficient attention has been paid to the special problems of organisation and administration thus created, they do exhibit many of the symptoms usually associated with the departments of state. And many qualified observers, while admitting the great economies possible with large-scale business combinations, have expressed doubts under this very head. The existence of such doubts is an added reason for an intensive examination of the methods of training administrators, by business men and educationalists acting in collaboration.

That such collaboration is essential appears immediately if the whole problem is regarded realistically. Whatever may be the case with other grades of workers the administrator does not spring armed *cap-à-pie* from the examination hall of his university or technical school. That he sometimes thinks he does is in some sort a criticism of the educational methods of these institutions, .but a criticism which has been very much overdone in certain business quarters. The business man who, at this juncture, undertakes the second stage of his training, should be at least prepared to deal humorously with a certain crop of intellectual wild oats. The fact that the soil is fertile enough for such casual growth is far more important than any slight trouble he may be put to in clearing it away. The persistence of these criticisms demonstrates, however, the necessity of emphasising that the man who at 35 or 40 succeeds to important administrative responsibilities in business is a joint product from the point of view of training. However far apart in understanding are those who have been concerned with his instruction up to that point, he remains an individual, a unity, and an individual whose fitness for his task is determined not by his formal academic education alone, nor by his subsequent business practice alone, but by the blending of these two experiences and their issue in a particular type of mind and character.

Education and training are processes which are continuous throughout life. And if the supply of future business leaders is ill-trained or inadequate it is of little avail for business men to accuse the Schools and Universities of sending them unsuitable material or for the schools and universities to charge business men with spoiling the material which they do send them. In so far as there is failure to solve the problem it is their joint responsibility, their mutual treachery to the future welfare of the community.

The tendency towards the specialisation of function within the structure of business which has been described in earlier chapters, places the educationalist in a dilemma. In a practical world his pupils expect to leave him equipped to start earning a livelihood immediately. On the other hand, in a world which is also competitive that demand tends to emphasise a form of training which is itself highly specialised and vocational in character. The young graduate must possess a store of marketable knowledge adequate to enable him to fill a subordinate position in some single one of the many sharply differentiated functions of a modern business.

At the same time the educationalist, if he is worthy of the name, knows very well that such vocational training if carried to extremes, is, whatever its immediate utility, unlikely to be the most suitable form of education taking the long view. Whatever the proficiency of his pupil in the immediate field it will have been dearly bought unless at the same time he has acquired a balanced view of the general contribution of other departments of knowledge to the common stock, not to mention intellectual habits which will enable him to approach tasks outside his own special field with intelligence and insight.

Within business itself the same dilemma occurs. Under the older forms of organisation where responsibilities were divided by departments or processes, the subordinate manager tended to come into personal contact with a wide variety of problems. Within his own area of responsibility he was supreme, dealing on his personal authority with personnel questions, technical matters, accountancy issues, the purchase of materials, and so on. But the necessity for specialisation in order to keep pace with the growing volume of scientific knowledge is forcing upon businesses in every direction a form of organisation where duties and responsibilities are divided by function . . . one department dealing with accountancy questions wherever they arise in the factory, another doing all the buying and so on.

Of the efficiency and economy of this second method there is no question. But it does remove from the developing executive, that training in the general problems of the business which, under the older form of organisation, he obtained automatically in the course of his daily work. The more efficient he is at his particular functional job the more likely he is to be advanced along that specialised line, to concentrate his theoretical studies and his practical activities on one aspect of the business. And this is so with regard even to the most important positions in the enterprise. A really brilliant Sales Manager is likely to remain on selling work.

If, however, the business is to maintain its supply of General Managers—men suitable to take sole charge of a branch factory or affiliated undertaking (a requirement thrown into prominence by the increasing number of amalgamations), this tendency will prove a source of weakness, unless the general training provided by the older form of organisation is deliberately replaced by special measures designed to broaden the individual's outlook and to give him a working acquaintance with functions other than his own. The nature of such measures is obvious. It includes suitable arrangements for the transfer of promising officials from function to function, opportunities for committee work on problems common to a number of functions, visits to other factories and to congresses and conventions, etc.

One of the greatest obstacles to the creation of any really satisfactory scheme for the training of future business leaders is the persistence of

an artificial distinction between what is called
" theoretical " and what is called " practical ".
This is largely due to the character of the change
which comes in a student's life when he leaves
school or college and " goes out into the world ".
The moment is dramatised, both to the student
and by his new superiors. He is thus led to distinguish sharply between his academic life and his
new experiences. Because, in the majority of cases,
examinations are behind him, he is only too prone
to imagine that the whole standards and apparatus
of conscious intellectual endeavour should be
jettisoned. The illiteracy of many successful business men in their own subject is remarkable. They
are successful in despite of it : not because of it.
But they help to maintain the myth that there is
a dividing line—on one side of it " practical " life
and on the other the " mere theories " of school-
men. And as long as that myth persists it will be
impossible to treat the subject of training for leadership as it should be treated—namely as a whole,
including both the academic education of those
concerned and the earlier stages of their careers in
business. It is suggested that while business men
have an obligation in this matter, it is an obligation
which extends to the educationalist. He must take
his share of the initiative in securing that the
necessary contacts are established and maintained.

In the light of this proviso, that the academic
portion of education for administration is only the
first part of one continuous process, it is possible
to consider the problems which more directly

trouble the educationalist. One of his biggest difficulties, the choice between a vocational and more general form of training, has been described. A second dilemma of the same character arises directly from specialisation of function. If, as has been suggested, it is more than a full-time job for an intelligent official to keep pace with the developments in any one function, it is clearly impossible for the administrator to be intimately acquainted with all of them. It is still more impossible for a student to acquire a useful amount of knowledge bearing on the whole series. It is suggested that it is a great weakness in the majority of courses in Commerce or Business Administration that they attempt to cover far too wide a field. The student has an insufficient knowledge of any one of his subjects to equip him effectively to earn his livelihood by practice in that department of business. At the same time he has insufficient practical acquaintance with economic life to fit into a working and coherent scheme the various doses of economics, commercial geography, commercial law, accountancy, scientific management and the like to which he has been exposed.

What appears to have happened in such cases is this, the educationalist for reasons already suggested has revolted, and rightly revolted, against the narrowness of a purely vocational and specialised curriculum. But at the same time he has felt compelled to compromise with the vocational conception to some degree. And consequently he has selected the whole of his material from the functions of business life or from subjects closely allied to them. Frequently the compromise has been carried a stage further—the preliminary examination for a degree involving a generalised study of various business subjects and the secondary stage permitting a partial specialisation directed towards a career in some definite branch of business activity, banking or export merchandising or industry, for example.

It is to be doubted whether this type of compromise fulfils either of the two main requirements of business. It certainly does not equip the student for immediate money-making as a subordinate in a particular function. Equally it does not appear proven that at its present stage business itself presents the type of material best suited to train the mind of the young student on lines which will fit him to assume the large administrative responsibilities which will be required of the business leader of the future.

The main ground for doubts of this character, and particularly with reference to current textbooks and examination syllabuses, is to be found in that comparative inexperience of business in tasks of large-scale administration which has already been emphasised. Because of this inexperience there has been hitherto comparatively little specific study of the function of administration considered separately from the technical activities which it is concerned to direct. Apart from Mr. Henri Fayol's distinguished work *L'Administration Industrielle et Generale* and a certain number of American publications, among which may be mentioned Mr. E. D. Jones' *Industrial Leadership and Executive Ability* and Mr. S. Lewisohn's *The New Leadership in Industry*, business men themselves have devoted little attention to the matter.

Undoubtedly there is still widely current an idea that leadership and administration cannot be taught save by experience. It is expressed in such phrases as " leaders are born, not made ", " that indefinable something which makes a man a leader of his fellows ", " that unanalysable quality which constitutes command ", and so on. But the growth of a professional attitude towards management and the development of the scientific standpoint in approaching its tasks has done a great deal to weaken the conviction with which such ideas are held. The scientist does not readily admit that any quality is unanalysable. The psychologist has only to be faced with an " indefinable something " in human nature to suspect a self-regarding complex.

Even, however, if the proposition that administration *can* be taught is accepted, that does not solve the problem of how it is to be taught. This raises immediately a second dilemma. It is clear that the ruling conception among those interested in management is the idea of dealing with every problem through the intellectual technique developed in the exact sciences. On the other hand it is undeniable that the majority of the problems which press for solution on the modern administrator are of an order " in which the human element is dominant ".

Experimental psychology and the physiology of the nervous system are supplying a certain modicum of exact knowledge on this subject. But, comparatively speaking, these are young sciences. And many decades are still required before a precise guidance in many vital administrative issues can be expected from them. While not neglecting the invaluable training and insight afforded by a study of their principles, the administrator must ultimately depend on human judgment in a wide variety of decisions. That is to say, if the view is accepted that a humanistic education confers power in the balancing of probabilities in which the human element is dominant, his training must include the humanities in some definite form.

On the other hand it is vitally necessary in dealing with groups of highly skilled specialists who are increasingly professionally conscious that such exercise of judgment should be, as far as possible, impersonal. The growth of the democratic spirit in the advanced industrial countries spells disaster for the leader in business who attempts to exercise a purely personal control. Men will accept much hardship and difficulty provided their intelligence is satisfied that it is inevitable, what one political scientist has called " the law of the situation ". They will accept nothing which is presented to them in the guise of the arbitrary will of another individual. It follows therefore that " self-elimination in forming a judgment "—the chief result of scientific training—is equally vital to the administrator.

Taking the long view, the need for the deliberate training of future administrators which has been outlined may well force business itself to alter fundamentally its whole conception of the right methods of intellectual development, not only with regard to matter, but also in respect of time and place. While business is short of experience in such questions, other institutions are not. And it is noteworthy that throughout the military and naval systems of the world, where that need has been most manifest, the integration of formal theoretical instruction with practical experience is worked out on a definite scheme extending far later into the life of the individual than is the case with other professions. Particularly to be remarked is the fact that in such institutions those who wish to rise to high command are practically compelled to devote one or two years at an intermediate stage of their career to advanced theoretical work of an exacting character at a staff college or Naval War School.

Moreover, such training is but the culmination of a process which has been continuous since the young officer first embarked on his career. Following on a good general education he is first trained specifically in the duties of his profession as they are presented to a subordinate executive. There follow eight or ten years of actual practice. But throughout this period he is forced to continue with some theoretical study both to pass certain qualifying examinations on which his promotion depends and as the result of " courses " intended to acquaint him with the special technique of branches of the service other than that in which he is personally engaged. Finally, his admission to the advanced instruction on which promotion to high administrative rank is dependent, is usually conditional on an unimpeachable record in practice plus success in a competitive examination, designed to prove that his general intellectual background is adequate to the tasks imposed by such advanced instruction.

A somewhat different parallel is offered by the medical profession. Medicine is still an art. But it is an art which uses the scientific method throughout its practice. It has traditionally an attitude towards the duty of training its next generation which survives as the finest heritage left by the apprenticeship system. Here the young entrant is not only required to possess a high level of general education. He is submitted to a process of training both theoretical and practical which is long and exacting. And once more the attainment of the minimum qualification legally required if he is to practice is not regarded as sufficient for more than a very undistinguished career. If he is to attain to the higher ranks of the profession he is expected to supplement an initial period of practical work with further theoretical study.

The development of a state of public opinion which will admit of such a type of continuous intellectual training for business administrators, is largely a matter for business men themselves. It must surely take time. And in the meanwhile the educationalist must content himself with the present bisected system, where the student sits like Humpty Dumpty on an academic wall till the end of his school or university career, and then falls with a crash into practical life—only too frequently, alas, to renounce its intellectual consideration for evermore. But the educationalist would be wise to keep in mind the possibility of a more balanced arrangement.

Even assuming the existing situation much can be done to improve academic training so that it approximates more closely to the real requirements of business.

In actual practice, while each entrant to business starts as a specialist in some one function, the great majority of successful men and women are successful because they pass over into general administration. The prizes of business as a whole fall to those who can get things done, that is to say, to those who can handle men. For each higher post open to the pure, specialist who lacks this faculty there are a dozen for the man with good knowledge and practical experience of one function of business who in addition is of the true executive type. The changes necessary to adjust existing systems of training more closely to this unquestionable reality are not very great. But they do involve a complete abandonment of that vocational compromise which underlies so many syllabuses.

The principle of such a system of training as is here contemplated is simple. It postulates for *each* student a thorough and detailed vocational preparation for some *one* of the major functions of business, whether it be in accountancy, engineering, statistics, marketing and distribution, chemistry, design, purchasing, or some other. Such training should be rigorously scientific both as to method and content. Apart from the knowledge of the detailed subject-matter of his special function it should leave in the student's mind a clear conception of the scientific intellectual technique, of its standards and of its discipline.

But in addition to this specialised training all students, whatever their function, should be required to undergo a supplementary course in administration. Preferably this course should follow on some period of actual work in business. Where this is not practicable, it should form the concluding portion of their undergraduate work. It should be conceived on the broadest possible lines with the intention, not so much of inculcating knowledge as of opening the windows of the mind, both on the past and towards the future. It should show something of notable administrative achievement in many walks of life and of the necessary interdependence of the principles on which all great administrators work. It would thus express one of the basic conceptions of humanism—" let us now praise famous men ". But it should touch too on the possibilities suggested by modern experimental psychology and personnel methods and by scientific public administration firmly based on correct statistical procedures.

It would admittedly be a difficult curriculum to frame and to administer : it would call for inspiration as well as knowledge in the teachers.

But the fact that it was generalised for all classes of entrants into business life, and would indeed be applicable also to candidates for posts in public administration, would widen the field of demand for it. This would involve not only larger resources, but also a more extensive area of experiment and experience.

Above all it would yield a type of recruit for business who would be to some degree prepared for the heavy and increasing responsibilities which await the administrator of today. Because, while his mind had been disciplined, rendered impersonal and objective, by the study of the things relating to his immediate function, it would have been balanced by an appreciation of the task which awaits those who would handle men. The economic history of the immediate past is one long record of disasters and misunderstandings due to a loss of that essential balance.

# XI

" A wise social control will accomplish its greatest and most lasting results by proper provision for the education of managerial leaders of the right type. Research and the application of research, scientific and economic, rather than entrepreneuring is the chief requirement of modern business."—H. A. MARQUAND, *The Dynamics of Industrial Combination*.

## CHAPTER XI

### THE TRAINING OF THE ADMINISTRATOR

WHILE the last chapter dealt primarily with the education, prior to entry into business, of the type of recruit likely to develop into a future administrator, the argument throughout was based on the assumption that a continuous process of training after the start of a business career was essential. Many undertakings have already given much attention to the more obvious intellectual aspects of this question.

But it is doubtful if the moral factors, the influences brought to bear on the recruit or young executive by the tone, standard of organisation, and personal reception which he meets within the enterprise have been appreciated at their full weight as factors in training. Above all there is some ground for suspicion that the effects exercised by the characteristics of the system of promotion have frequently been underestimated. Where a staff is convinced that advancement is, as far as is humanly possible, based on fitness and fitness alone in the interests of the service, that conviction is the most powerful single stimulus available to the administration in securing from all concerned conscious and continuous effort at self-development.

The difficulty of incorporating new entrants who are somewhat older than usual into any organisation is a real one. One well-known business leader has written that university graduates " have no knowledge of business. They are not specialised. They have no experience of handling men—which is most important. Business wants men who are accustomed to use men wisely." [1] A university graduate making his first start cannot be expected to have these qualities. He has not been engaged in acquiring them. Business should expect to teach him man management as the Army trains its young officers. What should be expected of him is that he will prove more adaptable, and quicker to learn the essential things than the elementary or secondary schoolboy. At the same time he probably has to be paid at the same rate as the man who, for the time being, is more valuable. It requires patience and foresight on the part of the employer to give the time, attention and money which are necessary.

The graduate, because he has been engaged on more advanced intellectual work, has frequently to sow some mental wild oats, before he gets into touch with realities. An employer, who has many university men in his organisation, has said " when a young man comes down from Oxford or Cambridge he has often certain fantastic ideas, and somebody has to relieve him of them ".[2] The same

[1] Sir Robert MacAlpine, *Evening Standard*, January 13th, 1927.
[2] Mr. Gordon Selfridge, *ibid.*, January 13th, 1927.

Evidence of a failure to appreciate this aspect of the problem is to be found in many directions, notably in the constantly recurring controversy as to whether university candidates are suitable for business. The Balfour Committee in discussing the cotton trade reported :

" Very few firms pay much attention to the pre-industrial training of the entrant, but if he shows promise after he has entered the mill most firms will give him opportunities. So strong and widespread is the opinion that to succeed he must enter at the earliest possible age and grow up in the actual practice of his trade, that practical experience is often regarded not merely as an essential part of his training, but even as the only training that matters." [1]

Apart from this exaggerated bias in favour of empiricism, criticism of university candidates is directed to three points. It is said that they lack the character, the habits and outlook suitable for business life. Emphasis is laid on the difficulties encountered in introducing men at a rather later age than that at which industry has been accustomed to take recruits. Doubts are expressed as to whether the actual intellectual equipment which results from university education is appropriate to commercial activities.

While, as was indicated in the preceding chapter, there may be some substance in the last point, the first two show a certain unreadiness on

[1] *Factors in Industrial and Commercial Efficiency*, p. 206, Part I of a Survey of Industries, Balfour Committee on Industry and Trade, London, 1927.

the part of industry to shoulder its fair share of the responsibility of training its future leaders.

Two published statements on the question of character read :

" If you get a man who has had no discipline except the university—which is more or less a club—and the other man has been up for several years against men of the world and has had all the rough edges knocked off him, it stands to reason that he is in a better position." [1]

and

" There appears to be widespread testimony that in the great majority of cases the class-instinct of the under-graduate of Cambridge or Oxford makes him difficult or impossible in business or industry." [2]

The recruit from a university, at the moment when he enters industry, cannot be as immediately useful in a subordinate capacity as the man who has been four or five years with the concern. But this short-period comparison of his utility is beside the point. In the case of the university recruit contact with hard knocks has been deliberately postponed in order to enable him to secure a more balanced and thorough intellectual development. In knowledge of business processes and in character he is, at the moment of entering business, inevitably less advanced than his contemporary from the elementary school. The real test of his training comes with time. Does he at 30 show less character than the boy who started business earlier in life ?

[1] Sir John Ferguson, *Evening Standard*, January 13th, 1927.
[2] C. F. G. Masterman, *ibid.*, January 11th, 1927.

The accusation of class superiority founded on this very fact. The elementary boy often appreciates more clearly than h that the university entrant has qualificatio capacities, which, if given a clear opportu development, will take him farther than around him. The university man's contempo are established in the concern, of proven There are many opportunities of giving a impression about a beginner who is new to customs and methods of the organisation, a from the start an isolated, or at least a conspicu figure.

In the absence of patient and understan leadership, he has little protection against delibe or unintentional prejudice. In some busine the tradition of competition between individu still lingers, and " playing for one's own hand is considered more admirable than accuracy statement. The man trained in the traditions a great public school and university usually fin it impossible, fortunately, to compete in this orde of activity. It would be well if those who alleg that university candidates lack the character fo business, would sometimes ask themselves whethe their own organisations are of a character to receive university men. The administration of British India has called for character above every other qualification, and the assumption of the very largest responsibilities at an age which business would regard as fantastic. The necessary staff has been found in large measure by the older universities.

idea was expressed at a conference on the subject organised by The American Management Association. " Most graduates of schools of business go out with a desire to swing the world by the tail. Therein lies their promise and therein lie many of the problems with which their employers are concerned." The same speaker supplied the real answer.

" But why not that attitude? Could there be a more serious indictment of any institution than that it sends out youngsters into the world without a maximum of ambition and desire to do a big job. Many of the difficulties and many of the shortcomings in connection with the early experience of graduates in business may be found in just that fact." [1]

Closely related to this whole problem is the system of selection for advancement within the organisation. No large institution can or should attempt to rely on one social group, one particular combination of educational and practical opportunities, for its supply of future administrators. The capacity for leadership in the best sense is too rare and too valuable to be neglected wherever it is manifest. Whether the young entrant be elementary schoolboy, secondary schoolboy or university graduate, whether he come from a palace or a slum, he may equally have the qualities of leadership in him. They are not the qualities which make for flexible and docile subordinates—

[1] Dean Gray, American Management Association, Committee Reports, Series No. 8, p. 8.

the type which are described in the United States as " Yes-Men ".

The task of selection is one of the most difficult which faces the chief in any enterprise. It is not sufficient for him to be unbiassed and just himself. He must convey the conviction of his disinterestedness in all considerations save the good of the concern to every person employed by it. A number of observers have commented on a certain weakness in British business in this respect. A speaker at Oxford a few years ago told an industrial conference that the only principle or organisation he had been able to discover in English industry was " Myself, my father, my son, and my wife's sister's nephew." A friendly American visitor has written :

" A tremendous drawback to effective business organisation in England is the habit of asking who you are, as opposed to the American inquiry as to what you are. In England the fact that you are the husband of the daughter of the Managing Director is apt to mean more than the fact that you have discovered a new process for smelting steel that cuts a quarter off the price of production." [1]

The individual tradition still lingers. There are many great businesses where the problem of promotion has been faced—even if there are some where it has not. The Managing Director of a world-famous house has said : " I have made it an invariable rule never to admit a relative into the Company." At least one form of patronage

[1] F. Plachy, *Britain's Economic Plight*, p. 71.

had been definitely renounced. In other concerns, there is a salary committee of the directors which settles advances among the higher-paid officials. But on the whole, even where a real endeavour is made to promote on merit and merit alone, the idea persists that the judgment of a single person in a responsible position is a sufficient assessment of what constitutes merit and what does not. And many subordinates are inclined to accept that view.

On the whole, however, there seems little likelihood that they will long continue to do so. The question of advancement is vitally important to the individual. If he has a spark of vitality in him, he is prepared to stand or fall on his own merits. But he does demand, and will demand with increasing insistence, that the method by which those merits are determined is as careful, impartial, and as free from the chances of time, place, and caprice as human ingenuity can make it.

One psychologist has written :

" Crimes have been committed in the name of ' judgment of human nature '. Too often, selection is a guessing contest. All of us like to think we are good judges of men. Years hence industrial executives will recall this calm assurance that each of us is a good judge of men and smile." [1]

The experiments on which he based this opinion are interesting. In one case, arrangements were made for thirteen leading industrialists from different companies to select the best salesman from

[1] W. D. Scott and R. C. Clothier, *Personnel Management*, p. 24.

a group of twelve men sent in by a single company. Each of the judges was of major rank and long experience, and prided himself on his ability in choosing men. Thirteen complete sets of records and references for each of the twelve candidates were prepared and given to the judges. Each of them was asked to interview these candidates separately, using what method or procedure he wished, and then to rank them in order of his preference. A similar ranking based on the candidates' actual sales figures was obtained from the Company who had supplied them. What was the result? Of the thirteen rankings given by the individual judges as correlated with the average of all their rankings, only five were better than 0 60; one was 0·11 and another 0·26. The man placed 10th by the Company found a judge to place him 2nd, and the man placed 2nd by the Company appeared 9th and 11th on two of the lists. Only three judges correlated better than 0·50 with the Company's ranking, while four correlated lower than 0·25.

It is not suggested that the task of selection for promotion among men whose work and personalities are in some degree known is quite the same problem as the choice of previously unknown candidates by means of records and interview. But in most large businesses, opportunities of promotion as they occur are usually provided by vacancies in another department or function of the concern. The manager of the new department frequently knows little of the real capacities and personality of the various candidates, except such impressions as he can gather from other managers. And these are all coloured not only by the personal idiosyncrasies of the manager making the selection, but, too, by those of the manager making the report, and by the past and present personal relations between the two managers.

It is necessary, too, that the interests of the Company as a whole should be represented in the transaction. Departmental interests and requirements should take second place to the more general issue of a contented staff and the maintenance of an adequate supply of candidates to fill positions of responsibility as vacancies arise.

While administrative technique is still far from a satisfactory solution of the problem, experiments have been made which indicate the lines of investigation. It is impossible to establish any adequate system of promotion in an enterprise of any kind, unless the form of the organisation is clearly determined. The necessary preliminary to selecting an individual for a post of any kind is a review of the duties, and responsibilities, which that post involves. Such a review is inadequate if it is arrived at in isolation for the special purpose of the appointment, or traditional and not reduced to definite set terms.

The first step therefore is a complete analysis of the duties and responsibilities of every job in the organisation. Such an analysis should be in standard form and should include particulars of the qualifications as to sex, age, education, experience, special skill and so on required for each post.

It should also show the positions above and below each job for which it qualifies the incumbent or from which it is in the normal line of promotion. From such particulars it is possible to construct a promotional chart showing all concerned the whole possibilities of each avenue of advancement, the specialised jobs which lead to a blind alley, the next position to work for, and so on.

In the present state of our knowledge it is quite impossible to escape from the factor of personal judgment or opinion in estimating the relative importance of various jobs, or in the selection of individuals to fill them. But when direction is forced to use individual judgment it can make a conscious effort to improve its impartiality. Just as science works by definition and analysis, so to this troublesome and unscientific guess-work these instruments can be applied. Supervision, for instance, is of many different kinds, exercised over different numbers of people at different levels of responsibility. These differences can be reduced to terms expressing the amount and kind of responsibility expected from the subordinate, and the amount and kind of oversight exercised by the superior at each level. The same is true of the personal qualities of an individual exercised within a job. The existence of the defined qualities serves to remind those responsible that they are *not* being asked to consider whether they like A's politics or dislike B's wife.

Deliberate analytic rating of this description if well-established as a periodic procedure has the added advantage that it reveals weaknesses both to rater and rated, the judge and the victim. Tendencies to hasty or superficial judgments are revealed in the periodic variations which record any inclination on a superior's part to give way to temporary impressions. On the other hand, if all ratings are, as they should be, shown to the individual concerned, he is able to see immediately in what aspects of skill or character he is least successful in the opinion of those above him— a valuable guide in securing self-improvement. Finally, these methods, since they deliberately aim at impartiality, can be used by committees trained in the technique far more effectively than the single nomination. It is difficult for any party or "interest" in a group deliberately to mark a man higher for a specific quality than others who are notoriously his superiors in that respect. Similarly, in settling the relative status of appointments or departments, analysis and definition, coupled with consensus of opinion round a committee table, iron out departmental claims and jealousies more quickly than any other device.

Much experiment in many different directions is required before the principles of this technique will be firmly established. But the methods sketched are themselves a valuable instrument of training both for subordinates and for those who assist in selection. They inculcate objectivity, the scientific spirit, in a matter which is one of the most fruitful sources of prejudice and emotional malaise in all forms of undertaking.

No aspect of management touches more closely upon the prospects of industrial civilisation than the problem of the training and selection of those who are to administer business. Upon its solution depend not only co-operation in the immediate present, but the ultimate acceptance or rejection by mankind of the machine technology as a way of life and culture. Submission to disciplines is essential to the machine processes. It will be achieved in so far, and only so far, as it can be reconciled with the desire and opportunity for spiritual freedom. And " man desires to be free, not in order to be spared tribulation—that is more liable to increase in proportion to the degree of self-determination attained—but in order to grow ".[1]

[1] Hermann Keyserling.

## XII

" Mankind is now in one of its rare moods of shifting its outlook. The mere compulsion of tradition has lost its force. It is the business of philosophers, students, and practical men to recreate and re-enact a vision of the world, conservative and radical, including those elements of reverence and order without which society lapses into riot, a vision penetrated through and through with unflinching rationality. Such a vision is the knowledge which Plato identified with virtue.

Epochs for which, within the limits of their development, this vision has been widespread are the epochs unfading in the memory of mankind. There is now no choice before us : either we must succeed in providing a rational co-ordination of impulses and thoughts, or for centuries civilisation will sink into a mere welter of minor excitements. We must produce a great age, or see the collapse of the upward striving of our race."—A. N. WHITEHEAD, Introduction to *Business Adrift* by W. B. Denham.

# CHAPTER XII

## CONCLUSION

THE aspects of business management considered in the preceding chapters have centred round four main questions.

Changes of industrial structure and methods imperatively demand a re-orientation of conceptions as to the control of economic affairs. Such recasting must be consistent with the scientific logic which underlies the discovery and development of the machine processes. Definition, analysis, measurement, synthesis and proof are the keys to every problem which face the world in the conduct of business enterprises. The approach in each instance should be objective and inspired with the spirit of research.

The effective working of any undertaking which requires the co-operation of human beings is largely dependent on organisation, the structure of duties and responsibilities allocated to individuals into which the total task is divided. The science of organisation is new. It requires much further expansion through the comparative study of institutions designed for different purposes and, particularly, in the field of business management, the organisation of the complex amalgamations which are increasingly typical of the time.

The present breakdown in the world's business affairs is largely due to a failure to adjust consumption and distribution to the potentialities of production. This breakdown could have been anticipated. The scientific control of production has been developed with accelerating speed for over a century. Distribution, and particularly the co-ordination of consumption and production, have been left to the hazards of uninformed competition. This problem and the difficulties to which it has given rise can only be resolved by the same intellectual processes which have yielded improved control of productive methods. In particular the individual manufacturer and trader should take deliberate steps to restore the intimate knowledge of consumer demand which was absorbed unconsciously by attendance at more primitive markets.

These things can only be brought about given a high standard of training and scientific enlightenment among all who occupy positions of responsibility in business. The education of foremen and supervisors is as necessary as the education of administrators. Without them the decisions of administrators, however appointed, cannot be implemented. The preparation of recruits for the higher ranks of the business hierarchy should be both scientific and humanist. But the influences brought to bear upon them after entering on their business careers are equally a part of their training. Research and experiment into methods of recruiting and promoting managers designed to secure the fullest expression for the qualities of leadership are urgently necessary.

These four questions, promotion of the scientific standpoint, organisation, distribution, and training for future control appear to the author to be attracting most attention and to be the subject of the most earnest enquiry among serious students of business management throughout the world. It is likely that in all these matters the near future will witness a widespread and progressive modification of previous ideas and practice as the result of a growing volume of research.

There are two other issues, not specifically included in this book, which are equally susceptible to scientific treatment.

Not only has the distribution of goods and services been allowed to develop without any scientific enquiry into the processes involved at all commensurate with the attention paid to production. In addition the monetary mechanisms on which trade and industry depend for their vehicle of exchange have received little study of an engineering description. Of currency theories there are a plethora. Of detailed analyses of the actual functions of different types of financial institution, of their cost, and of the service rendered in relation to that cost there are fewer.

As was pointed out in Chapter VII the work done by financial institutions is essentially facilitative. It is secondary to the main purpose of the economic system which is to produce and to distribute goods and services. But the accidents of an uncontrolled evolution have placed those whose function it is to direct and to control monetary policy in an exceptionally strong position in relation to manufacturers and to traders. The present chaos of the world's loan and exchange position offers at least a suggestion that the traditional monetary system is not as well adapted as in the past to handle the needs of a rapidly developing mechanical production.

The subject has not been closely considered in this book owing to the conviction that in dealing with currency as in dealing with a factory, the scientific method can only achieve full results when it is applied by responsible people from within rather than by students of the subject from without. The rapid mechanisation of banking and insurance operations should secure the growth of a class of financial managers who are acquainted with the outlook of scientific management. Interest in modern techniques in accountancy and office control in relation to the work of financial institutions has undoubtedly expanded in recent years. But these activities are comparatively subsidiary considered in relation to the main lines of interest in large-scale financial operations. Only responsible individuals widely experienced in monetary institutions, fully seized with the " mental revolution " which F. W. Taylor postulated, and of an originality and executive capacity to break with current conventions, to review the situation as a whole afresh and to embark on experiments, are likely to do effective work in this field. Possibly the greatest obstacle to rapid development is the fact that the vast majority of those engaged in financial business are in a fiduciary position. Such a position does not encourage experiment.

There is, however, little doubt that the possibilities of a scientific management of financial facilities will be explored with increasing interest at no very distant date. Already those who feel the immediate impact of the machine technology are in process of revolutionising their financial methods and conceptions. The control of manufacturing operations in terms of money has, since the beginning of this century, been profoundly modified in the direction of greater precision and more refined information. Detailed costing of manufacturing processes is a commonplace. Practical methods of costing distributive operations are now available, though not as yet in general use. The conception of statistical forecasts of the trend of general trade and monetary influences as a substitute for personal judgment as to future tendencies is widely accepted. It is not to be anticipated that financial institutions will be unaffected by so widespread a tendency.

Much, however, remains to be done. In the disposition of the surplus yielded by manufacturing industry decisions are still largely empirical and traditional. The handling of capital is, it is to be presumed, one of the cardinal questions of policy in a so-called " capitalist " system. But the actual decision as to the use to be made of any surplus still depends, in the majority of cases, on the product of various influences and conventions, rather than on a scientific survey of the facts.

In recent years a distinction has been drawn between the need for the replacement of equipment due to wear and tear (depreciation) and the same need when caused by rapid technological development (obsolescence). But, in the vast majority of cases figures are lacking as to the amount of capital investment in any given industry required to keep one worker in employment or as to the volume and speed of change in that figure. Similarly the relation between general purchasing power and the earnings of particular groups of workers remains a matter of opinion rather than of exact measurement. It is probable that an increased volume of management research will be directed to these and other similar questions in the future.

Finally, the spread of Rationalisation and the results achieved by the closer integration of various industries and of some national economies, have directed attention to the possibility of a more deliberate planning and co-ordination of economic life both nationally and internationally. A large-scale experiment in this order is in process in Russia. But the opinion is gaining ground in a number of the older industrialised countries that there is no essential connection between more planning and the particular form of socialist economy which has been adopted by the Union of Socialist Soviet Republics. Speculation centres round the possibility of a free economy, on which nevertheless certain elements of conscious planning have been superimposed under the authority either of the State or of *ad hoc* bodies created by business itself for this purpose.

The conception of planning is of course inherently in line with the principles of Scientific Management. But, the experience already gained in planning within individual enterprises indicates that the acceptance of the idea is the least part of the process. Planning is essentially a technical issue, dependent for its success or failure, indeed for the possibility of its application at all, on the availability and accuracy of the necessary figures and on the skill with which they are used.

It is probably not an exaggeration to suggest that in none of the older industrialised countries, and in relation to no single industry within those countries, are there at present available the information and the mechanisms which would permit the immediate formulation of a practicable plan. On the other hand, the statistics and experience in the possession of a large number of uncoordinated agencies, both public and private, represent a larger proportion of the necessary basis than is commonly supposed.

The immediate task would appear to be the bringing together of these various resources and skills, and the objective and meticulous examination of what material for planning is actually available. If this could be done scientifically in the case of one or two typical industries, the results of such experiments would provide a valuable guide as to the possibility of more extensive developments.

But planning as a slogan, divorced from the conceptions of scientific management and its growing experience of planning technique in individual undertakings, might do untold mischief.[1]

Theories, whether capitalist or communist, fascist or socialist, individual or collective must all alike yield to the discipline of facts.[1] Man can create power by the hundred thousand horse. He can travel at immense speeds by land and sea and air. He can make two ears of corn grow where one grew before. He can speak with the Antipodes. But he can do these things for one reason and one reason only. Somewhere and somewhen men with a passion for knowledge for its own sake have toiled with patient, objective, accurate observation and measurement to win an understanding of some corner of natural process. They have been tortured, outcast and reviled. But they have persisted, until in this and that endeavour the world has learned to forget its myths and its superstitions, to adjust its action simply and rationally so that it is in alliance with nature and not in conflict with it.

Man is as much a part of nature as any other animal. Pasture and water, climate and

[1] Cf. " It is necessary to mention one general premise for social economic planning. . . . The plan . . . cannot base its methodology on anything else but science—the quintessence of social thought and experience."—Report of Mr. V. V. Obolensky-Ossinski, chief of the Soviet delegation, on *Social and Economic Planning in the Union of Socialist Soviet Republics* (Material presented to the World Congress on Social and Economic Planning, Amsterdam, August, 1931).

surroundings, the material bases of existence have determined the structure of his societies and the characteristics of his culture. He speaks of pastoral peoples and agricultural peoples. Today the nations of Christendom are machine peoples. But in many of their customs and methods of thought they seek to maintain the social structure and the culture evolved under an earlier and differing technique. This, fundamentally, is the cause of the maladjustments in their economic order. They are maladjustments which can be cured by one method and one method only, exactly as any other form of disease can be cured, the gradual winning of clearer knowledge by the processes of science. Scientific Management is but an affirmation that the problems of business management will yield only to these same processes of science. They will not yield to theories.

In this book an attempt has been made to outline some of the aspects of business in which research is most urgently needed, to suggest possible lines and methods of approach. Rationalisation has expanded and is expanding. Casual abuses of one or other of its findings are of passing significance. The events of recent years have proved conclusively that the individual enterprise which encounters its difficulties in the scientific spirit is better equipped than its fellows for the struggles of a competitive economy. But this again is a temporary consideration. More important, their experiments will contribute to knowledge, to a clearer understanding of the outlines of the new society which man must build if he is to live on terms with a mechanical technology.

What new forms will be evolved by business and science working in co-operation it is yet too early to say. Knowledge of the facts is insufficient. Thought and experiment are alike hampered by outworn conventions and traditional practices. One thing is certain. They will bear little resemblance either to the forms of the past or to the imaginative structures which theorists have tried to force upon the world. They will be sound and enduring on two conditions only. They must be intellectually consistent with the principles which underlie the achievements of machine production. They must be practically valid, mixed in the crucible of fact and cast in the mould of effective action.

# INDEX

Printed in Great Britain by Butler & Tanner Ltd., Frome and London

# HISTORY OF MANAGEMENT THOUGHT

*An Arno Press Collection*

Kirkman, Marshall M[onroe]. **Railway Revenue.** 1879

Kirkman, Marshall M[onroe]. **Railway Expenditures.** 1880

Laurence, Edward. **The Duty and Office of a Land Steward.** 1731

Lee, John. **Management.** 1921

Lee, John, editor. **Pitman's Dictionary of Industrial Administra-tion.** 1928

McKinsey, James O. **Managerial Accounting.** 1924

Rowntree, B. Seebohm. **The Human Factor in Business.** 1921

Schell, Erwin Haskell. **The Technique of Executive Control.** 1924

Sheldon, Oliver. **The Philosophy of Management.** 1923

Tead, Ordway and Henry C. Metcalfe. **Personnel Administration.** 1926

Urwick, L[yndall]. **The Golden Book of Management.** 1956

Urwick, L[yndall]. **Management of Tomorrow.** 1933